ORGAN
IMPROVISATION

A PRACTICAL APPROACH TO CHORALE ELABORATIONS FOR THE SERVICE

BY GERHARD KRAPF

AUGSBURG PUBLISHING HOUSE · MINNEAPOLIS, MINNESOTA

ORGAN IMPROVISATION

A Practical Approach to Chorale Elaborations for the Service

Manufactured in the United States of America

For my wife, Trudl

FOREWORD

The art of improvisation—spontaneously developing and embellishing musical thoughts—was already practiced in the early Renaissance. In the Baroque era it had reached its heights, both in ornamentation of vocal melodies and, more strictly, in instrumental forms. Whereas this technique in the nineteenth century served mostly as a means of demonstrating virtuosity, a new trend in our time returns to loftier aims, especially in Protestant liturgical music.

Until now there has been no published guide to improvisation. This book, though scholarly and well organized, is not a text book. There are no rigid rules; rather, there are suggestions supported by a wealth of examples, and in the later chapters there are even complete compositions in a highly personal idiom. No theories are offered. Practical orientation prevails. Considerable background is necessary, but the emphasis is placed on the student's continuous search. It is this search, not the achievement of goals and comfort, which, in the words of Arnold Schonberg, is essential.

The author's religious philosophy pervades the book. The Lutheran church has a rich heritage in the chorale. The chorale contains intellectual and emotional features which are utilized in the presentation of the Word. The texts, even if they are not always biblical have liturgical significance. The melodies too serve devotion, whether they are sung or presented by the organ which occupies a central position in the musical service. Like the words, these melodies are subjective in their emotional content, and objective to elaboration which might be improvisatory. Music of this type helps to recapture the unity between the composer and the congregation, once achieved in the time of J. S. Bach. Style and means are different today but the new organ movement of our century points in the same direction.

Every section of this study reveals that the author, my friend and former student, is not a theorist but always creative in composition and performance. As this book shows, he is also a teacher of rare gift. Most important, he never loses sight of the essentials: the spiritual and religious aspects of music. May his book have its well deserved success!

PAUL A. PISK

St. Louis, Missouri
June, 1966

PREFACE

This book is designed to provide a systematic approach to the study and teaching of organ improvisation. It is aimed specifically at the needs of service playing, and thus it stresses the practical aspects of chorale and hymn improvisation. While it does not claim comprehensive coverage or universal methodology, it has produced good results in the classroom. The chorale and hymn preludes given in the text as musical examples will also be of practical value for service playing.

Acknowledgments are due to:

Miss Sarah Hanks, whose faithful editing and typing assistance and whose many intelligent suggestions have been of invaluable aid;

Miss Ruth Olson, Editor of the Music Department of Augsburg Publishing House, whose patience and circumspection have been greatly appreciated;

the Graduate School of the University of Iowa, for personal encouragement and material assistance.

GERHARD KRAPF

Iowa City, Iowa
September 12, 1966

TABLE OF CONTENTS

Part One
PRELIMINARY KEYBOARD SKILLS

Chapter 1

BASIC TECHNIQUES OF HYMN PLAYING

The selection of exercises comprising Part One has been compiled for the benefit of the student wishing to practice basic skills. It is intended to present in outline form a practical review of the indispensable prerequisites for the study of improvisation. The material may be amplified, abridged, or even omitted altogether at the discretion of the teacher.

1. Play at sight Examples I_1 through I_3:

    (a) without pedal;

    (b) bass line with pedal;

    (c) soprano as *cantus firmus* in pedal (4′ only), alto, tenor, and bass in the manual;

    (d) soprano as *cantus firmus* in right hand (solo registration), alto and tenor in left hand (accompaniment registration), bass in pedal.

2. Transpose at sight Examples I_1 through I_3 a major second up and down, using all techniques specified in (1a)–(1d).

Hymn tune "Das alte Jahr"

Michael Praetorius (1609)
Setting, G. K.

Ex. I_1

Hymn tune "Herr Christ, der einig Gotts Sohn"

Setting, Samuel Scheidt

Ex. I_2

Hymn tune "Gib Fried, o frommer, treuer Gott"

Setting, Samuel Scheidt

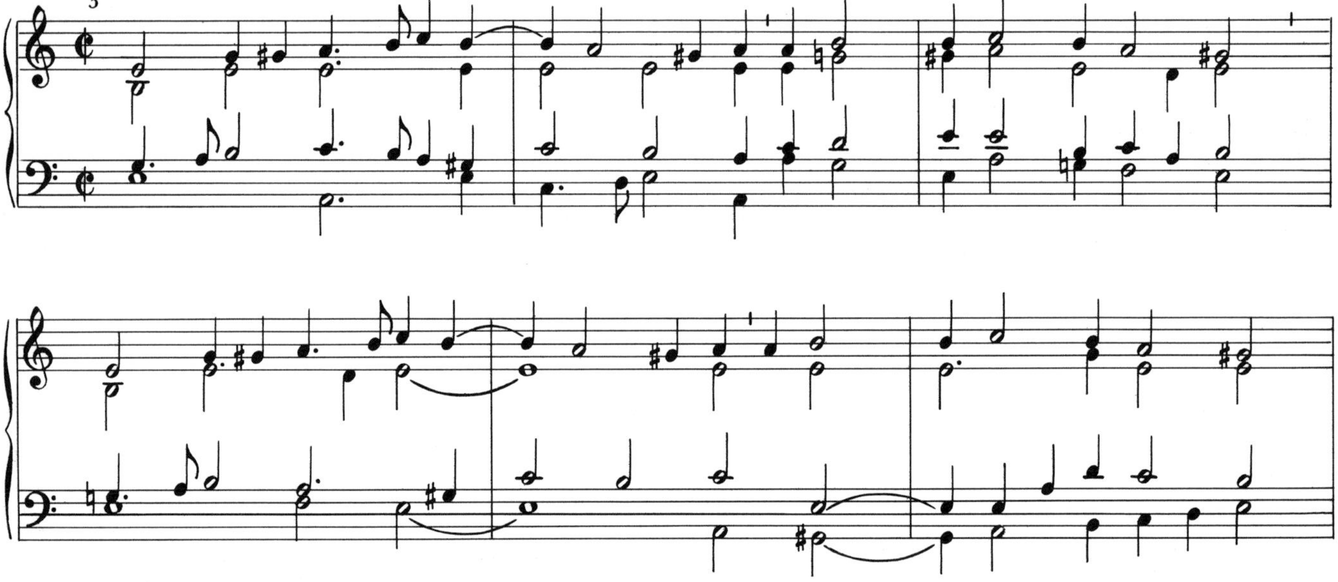

Ex. I 3

taken from: Samuel Scheidt, *Das Görlitzer Tabulaturbuch* (1650). Ed. Christhard Mahrenholz. New York, N.Y.: C. F. Peters, copyright 1941. Reprinted by permission.

3. Use hymnal and/or Scheidt's *Görlitzer Tabulaturbuch* for further practice. (See Selected Bibliography at the conclusion of Part One)

4. Play at sight Examples I_4 through I_6:

   (a) on one manual;

   (b) as a trio with bass in pedal;

   (c) with *cantus firmus* in pedal (4′ only), bass and inner voice on one or two manuals (left hand possibly with 16′ registration).

5. Transpose at sight Examples I_4 through I_6 a major second up and down, using all techniques specified in (4a)–(4c).

Hymn tune "Lobt Gott getrost mit Singen"

15th Century
Setting, G. K.

Ex. I $_4$

Hymn tune "Gelobt sei Gott"

Melchior Vulpius (1609)
Setting, G. K.

Ex. I₅

Hymn tune "Erhalt uns, Herr"

(1543)
Setting, G. K.

Ex. I₆

6. For further practice, the student is referred to three-part settings listed in Appendix II-B; see also Examples II₂₃a and II₂₄a.

7. Play at sight Example I₇:

  (a) on one manual;

  (b) inner voice as pedal *cantus firmus* (8′), outer voices on one or two manuals.

8. Transpose at sight Example I₇ a major second up and down, using the techniques specified in (7a) and (7b).

Hymn tune "Jesu, meine Freude"

Ex. I₇

F. W. Zachow

taken from: Friedrich Wilhelm Zachow, *Gesammelte Werke*. Ed. Max Seiffert, rev. Hans Joachim Moser; *Denkmäler Deutscher Tonkunst, XXII*. Wiesbaden: Breitkopf & Härtel, copyright 1958. Reprinted by permission.

9. For further practice, the student should play on the pedal relatively slowly-moving tenor, alto, and descant *cantus firmi* of chorale preludes that are notated on two staffs only. (Ample reference material is listed in Appendix II-C.)

5

Chapter 2

BASIC DRILLS IN KEYBOARD HARMONY

A. Harmonization of Melodies.

　1. Harmonize by sight in three and four parts, with and without pedal, Examples I_9 through I_{18}. Use simple chordal textures as shown in Example I_8. Try to apply the following suggestions:

　　a. Some common notes may be sustained (see alto, bars 1 and 2 of Example I_8b), others may be struck anew (see tenor in bar 2 and alto in bar 3 of Example I_8b) in order to achieve pleasing metric distribution.

　　b. Use contrary motion for root position progressions between adjacent triads (see bar 3 of Example I_8b).

　　c. Avoid excessive repetitiveness. Note how the bass leap of a seventh breaks the repetitive element of five successive six-chords (bar 1 and 2 of Example I_8a).

　　d. Where feasible, assign two (or more) chord functions to one note.

　　e. Choice of doubling should be decided by the criterion of smooth and interesting voice-leading.

　　f. Follow a mentally prepared outline of chord functions.

　　g. Attempt several alternative solutions for each exercise.

Ex. I_8　(a) Three-part harmonization

(b) Four-part harmonization

Ex. I_9　(a) Three-part harmonization

(b) Four-part harmonization

6

Ex. I₁₀

Ex. I₁₁

Ex. I₁₂

Ex. I₁₃

Bass lines

Ex. I₁₄   (a) Three-part harmonization

(b) Four-part harmonization

Ex. I₁₅

Ex. I₁₆

Ex. I₁₇

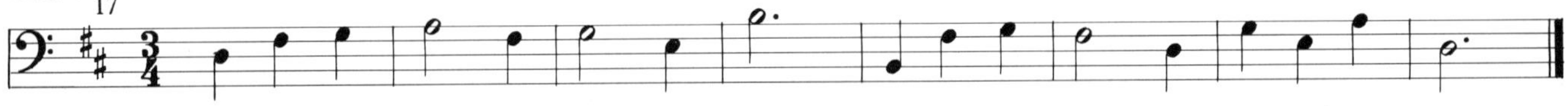

Ex. I₁₈

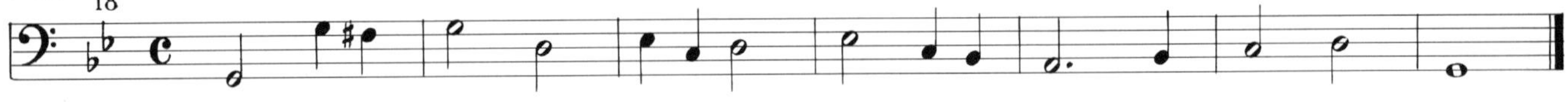

2. Using each of the phrases given in Examples I₂₀ through I₂₉ successively as soprano, alto (or tenor), and bass, add two and three parts at sight, as demonstrated in Example I₁₉a–I₁₉g. Begin using non-harmonic tones at your own discretion. Apply all techniques of playing as discussed in Chapter One. For additional practice, devise your own exercises by paraphrasing lines selected from suitable hymns (see Appendix I).

Ex. I₁₉ (a)   adapted from Bergamasca

(b)

Ex. I₂₃

Ex. I₂₄

Ex. I₂₅

Ex. I₂₆

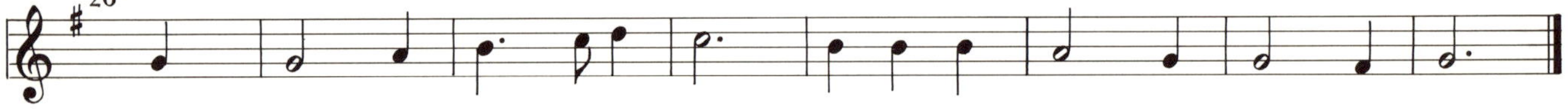

Ex. I₂₇

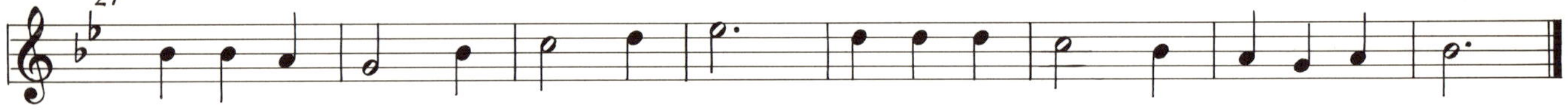

Ex. I₂₈

Ex. I₂₉

B. Simple Modulations.

A triad yields various possibilities as a pivot chord for modulations. The major triad C-E-G, for example, may be considered: C: I; G: IV; F: V; a: III; e: VI. The minor triad C-E♭-G may be considered: c: I; g: IV; B♭: II; A♭: III; E♭: VI. These possibilities can be realized by logical follow-up cadences (see Examples I₃₀ and I₃₁), in the manner suggested here.

PIVOT	FOLLOW-UP CADENCE
I	VI-IV-V-I
IV	V-VI-IV-V-I
V	VI-IV-V-I
II	III-IV-V-I
III	VI-IV-V-I
VI	IV-I$_4^6$-V-I

Ex. I₃₀

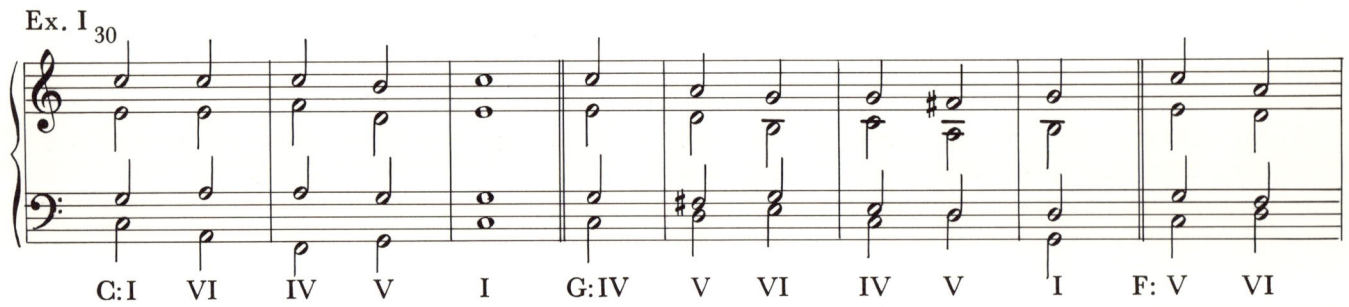

C:I   VI   IV   V   I   G:IV   V   VI   IV   V   I   F:V   VI

10

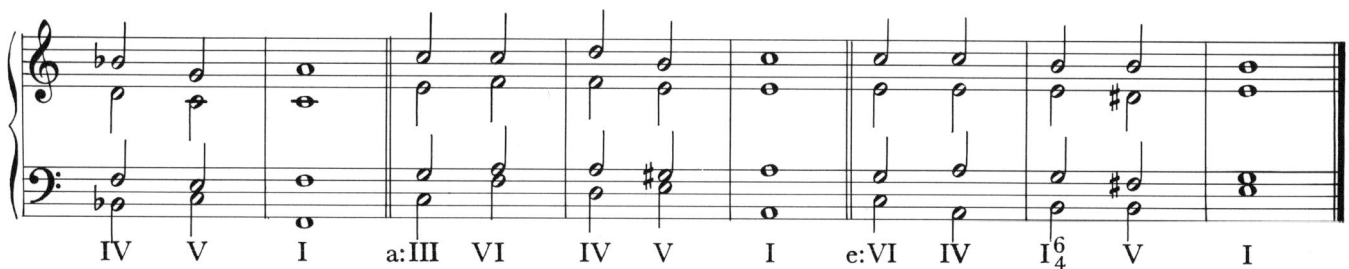

IV V I a:III VI IV V I e:VI IV I$^6_4$ V I

Ex. I$_{31}$

c:I VI IV V I g:IV V VI IV V I B♭:II III

IV V I A♭:III VI IV V I E♭:VI IV I$^6_4$ V I

1. Beginning with each of the twelve (enharmonic) major and minor triads, transpose the patterns shown in Examples I$_{30}$ and I$_{31}$ (each pattern is to be played in twelve different keys!); use various positions (root, third, fifth in soprano of opening chord; close and open harmony).

At your discretion, begin using chord inversions, seventh chords, non-harmonic tones, and freer voice-leading. Devise various alternate forms of follow-up cadences.

2. For each of the Examples I$_{32}$–I$_{47}$, play five modulations in the form of short, corresponding follow-up phrases, in two-part texture (see Examples I$_{32}$ and I$_{35}$), in three-part texture (see Examples I$_{33}$ and I$_{36}$), and four-part texture (see Examples I$_{34}$ and I$_{37}$). The pivot possibilities (see above) for Example I$_{34}$ are: C: I^6; G: IV^6; F: V^6 (non-modulating home key); a: III^6; e: VI^6. For Example I$_{37}$ the pivot possibilities are: e: I; b: IV; D: II; C: III; G: VI; etc.

Having gained confidence and facility, play the same examples again, this time adding one or two corresponding phrases of remodulation (see [a] in Example I$_{32}$).

Ex. I₃₂

(a)

F: V

C: I⁶

Ex. I₃₃

C: I⁶

Ex. I₃₄

C: I⁶

Ex. I₃₅

e: I

Ex. I₃₆

e: I

Ex. I₃₇

e: I

The foregoing chapters are intended to aid the student in reviewing his knowledge and development of basic skills in practical harmony. It must be stressed that complete mastery of the material in this section is imperative for the successful study of Part Two of this book. Students in need of further preliminary study are referred to the Selected Bibliography below.

SELECTED BIBLIOGRAPHY

Johnson, David N. *Instruction Book for Beginning Organists.* Minneapolis, Minn.; Augsburg, 1964, Chap. 22.

Keller, Hermann. *Schule der Choralimprovisation.* Leipzig: C. F. Peters, Pref. 1939, Chap. 1.

Lieberman, Maurice. *Keyboard Harmony and Improvisation,* 2 vols. New York: Norton, 1957.

Scheidt, Samuel. *Das Görlitzer Tabulaturbuch vom Jahre 1650.* Ed. Christhard Mahrenholz. Leipzig: Peters, 1941.

Part Two

THE IMPROVISED ELABORATION

Chapter 1

INTRODUCTION

Keyboard improvisation is as old as independent organ playing. The sparsity of early collections of organ music as well as the didactic character of such sources as Paumann's or Buchner's *Fundamenta* suggests that the larger part of organistic practice during the fifteenth and sixteenth centuries was improvisation. Even during the seventeenth and eighteenth centuries when manuscript collections and printed music had become commonplace, improvisation was considered an indispensable facet of an organist's training.

It is not within the scope of this book to trace and discuss the development of this musical discipline through the nineteenth and early twentieth centuries. Suffice it to say that in the wake of the eighteenth century Enlightenment, liturgical improvisation was gradually displaced by an admittedly extra-liturgical type of dazzling concert extemporizing.[1] The era of the *character piece* seems to have influenced to some extent even such master organists and composers as Mendelssohn and Bruckner, whose powers of improvisation were described by their contemporaries invariably in programmatic terms. Predominance of orchestral concepts applied to organ sound resulted in a pseudo-orchestral idiom; it depended heavily on homophonic textures that lent themselves well to the foundation-stop instrument.[2]

Although improvisation within the service never entirely ceased to exist, it needed to be re-examined. The *organ movement* and a growing liturgical awareness beginning in the late twenties have resulted in renewed emphasis on this important aspect of organistic practice.

While basic concepts and techniques of good improvisation are identical in kind for concert purposes as well as for use in the service, the present study will be limited to the latter. The guiding objective is to provide broadly applicable methods and principles of practical value for the church organist. Since the immediate liturgical occasion for improvisation is often hymn-related[3], most of the musical examples are based on chorales and hymn tunes.

Obviously certain prerequisites for the successful study of the art of improvisation must be assumed; the beginner should have a working knowledge of

Harmony: to the extent of being able to play by sight two-, three- and four-part harmonizations to given lines (including modal melodies), to play modulations (diatonic, chromatic, enharmonic) based on simple motifs and organized in recognizable formal structures (periods, symmetrical and asymmetrical phrases);

Counterpoint: to the extent of being able to analyze and practically apply the practices of eighteenth century instrumental counterpoint;

Formal Analysis: to the extent of complete understanding of the elements of musical forms and their structural characteristics;

Contemporary Music: to the extent of being able to analyze as large as possible a number of contemporary idioms and of being willing to understand contemporary composers on their own terms.

---

[1]A rather amusing account of such an improvisation by Georg Joseph Vogler is found in Mozart's letter to his father (written in Mannheim, Dec. 18, 1777): ". . . he is no more than a trickster *(Hexenmeister)*. The instant he attempts to play in a somewhat dignified *(majestätisch)* manner, he gets dry. One is relieved that he becomes impatient with it and cuts it short. But what follows after that?—an unintelligible babbling *(Gewäsch)*." Matthaei relates that Vogler was celebrated by enthusiastic audiences throughout Europe for his literally descriptive improvisations on such topics as "The pleasure cruise on the Rhine with intervening thunderstorm." (See Karl Matthaei, *Vom Orgelspiel*. Wiesbaden: Breitkopf & Härtel, 2nd rev. ed., 1949; p. 235.)

[2]For a broad discussion of some vital aspects concerning the relationship between idiom and type of instrument, see John Fesperman's book *The Organ as Musical Medium*. New York: Coleman-Ross, 1962, Chap. 5.

[3]See Gerhard Krapf, *Liturgical Organ Playing*. Minneapolis: Augsburg Publishing House, 1964, pp. 15ff. and p. 21.

It is true, these prerequisites amount in effect to requirements generally to be fulfilled by candidates for the bachelor's degree in music, indeed to some extent by candidates for graduate degrees. However, the attempt to acquire the ability to improvise freely *without* the benefit of sound training in the aforementioned disciplines will lead at best to rather rough, unpolished, sometimes "lucky" and momentarily deceptive, but ultimately undesirable results—at the worst, to hopeless groping and quite embarrassing, aimless rambling. Nothing could be less desirable within the framework of worship. It must be stressed, therefore, that the study of improvisation might well have to be preceded by a refresher course in keyboard harmony[4] or in one of the other disciplines mentioned. Patience and perseverance, however, will eventually be rewarded by success, for experience has shown that the mechanics of improvisation can be learned through industrious efforts. Musical talent certainly will be of immeasurable advantage in the creative application of these basic tools, but the acquisition of fundamental requirements is as necessary for the highly gifted person as it is for the student with average talent.

---

[4]For excellent review materials, see Selected Bibliography at the conclusion of Part I.

Chapter 2

BASIC TOOLS

There are a number of specific and immediately applicable skills which the beginner should acquire through systematic practice.

1. The first of these is the ability to "translate" directly into fluent lines on the keyboard a mentally preconceived skeletal harmonization of a given hymn.[5] (Examples II₁a–II₁c).

Hymn tune "Wach auf, wach auf, du deutsches Land"

Ex. II₁   (Hymn as placed on music rack)   Johann Walter (1561)

(a) Skeletal harmonization

(b) "Translation" into two-part texture

---

[5]For this and similar exercises as well as for the improvisation of hymn preludes or free accompaniments, it is suggested that the melody line be written out and placed on the music rack as a point of orientation. This relatively unfamiliar hymn tune has been chosen in order to avoid involuntary eclecticism.

(c) And into three-part texture

2. Translation of the skeletal shape of the *cantus firmus* into a florid line is another tool of improvisation. Accompanimental parts may be chordally oriented (Example II₂a) or relatively florid (Example II₂b) depending on the specific artistic intention of the organist.[6]

Ex. II₂   (a) c.f.

Sw.

Pos.

Ped.

(b) c.f.

[6]Analytical study of Pachelbel's chorale partitas is particularly rewarding with respect to a demonstration of a variety of possibilities which this simple and uncomplicated treatment can yield. (See Johann Pachelbel, *Sieben Choralpartiten, Ausgewählte Orgelwerke*. Ed. Karl Matthaei. Kassel: Bärenreiter, 1936.)

It will be noted that Examples II₁b and II₂b share the same bass line. While this is not mandatory, it is recommended for practice as an additional discipline. The student should practice the playing of various, distinctly different lines over identical basses as well as below identical descants.

3. After considerable practice and upon attaining a fair degree of fluency, the rendering of *cantus firmus* lines in inner voices should be added to these preliminary exercises (Examples II₃a and II₃b).

4. It is apparent that the harmonic outline in Examples II₃a and II₃b had to be altered in order to accommodate the *cantus firmus* in the inner voice. The harmonic scheme will be affected even more drastically when the *cantus firmus* is assigned to the bass. Exercises in which the *cantus firmus* bass line is played alternately by pedal and left hand are indispensable (Examples II₄a and II₄b).

5. Excepting Examples II₂a and II₂b, the *cantus firmus* line so far has been quoted literally. Quite frequently, however, a certain amount of melodic and rhythmic paraphrasing or reshaping of the *cantus firmus* will be necessary in order to adapt it to the overall texture chosen for a given improvisation. Example II₅ shows a few of such *cantus firmus* variants. The student should write additional variants of his own invention.[7]

6. The *cantus firmus* derivative is an important tool for various techniques of chorale improvisation (see Chapter 7). The student should practice deriving from given *cantus firmus* lines (see Appendix I) short motives (Examples II₆a and II₆b) as well as extended phrases (Example II₆c).

[7]For this and similar exercises, suitable material may be found in Appendix I or may be derived from any number of appropriate hymns.

7. Such derivations by themselves mean relatively little unless they are immediately tested for their usefulness. Example II$_6$a can be utilized through systematic application to a simple fundamental chordal scheme, as can Example II$_6$b (Examples II$_7$a and II$_7$b).

A note of caution must be sounded regarding too rigid and too repetitious use of motives. Example II$_7$b certainly tries the endurance of the listener to the breaking point.

Longer phrases, such as Example II$_6$c, may serve well as introductory passages, material for interludes between *cantus firmus* quotations or even fugue subjects (see Chapter 7). For the present time the student should practice quick memorization of such phrases, transposing from memory to different intervals (Examples II$_8$a and II$_8$b) as well as to related keys (Example II$_8$c), and improvising counterpoints to the phrases (Example II$_8$d).

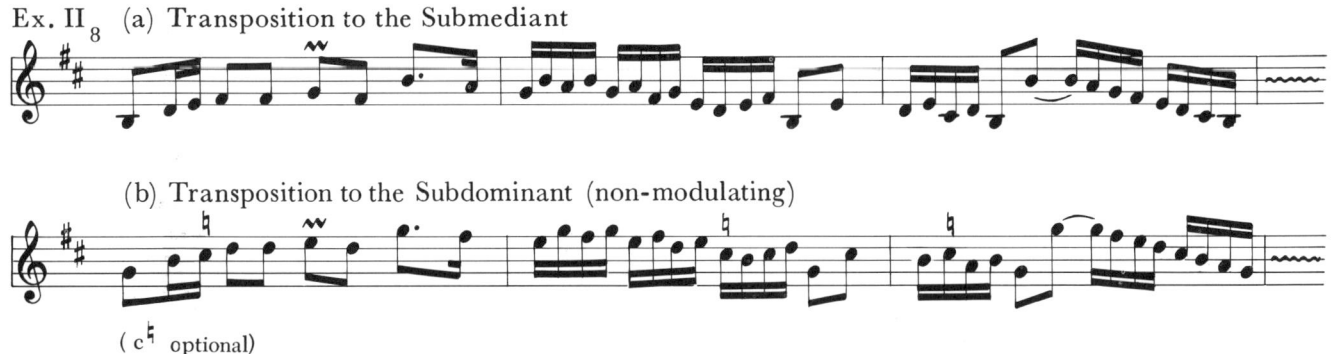

(c) Transposition to the Dominant key (*i.e.* modulating)

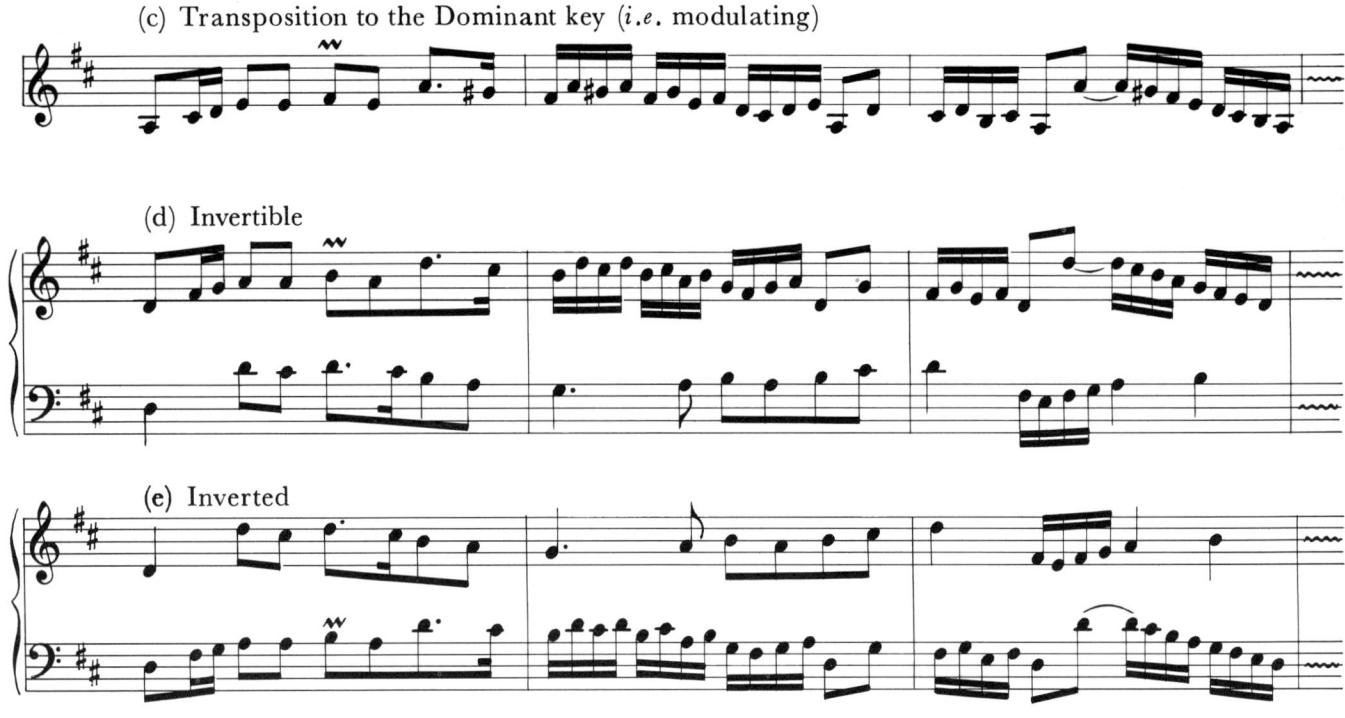

(d) Invertible

(e) Inverted

8. The ability to commit to memory instantly entire phrases and to form a quick mental perception of their possibilities for contrapuntal manipulation are two of the most important aspects of improvisation. Systematic and industrious practice is the only way to achieve mastery of them. Another closely related procedure is imitation, which in its strictest mode amounts to canonic formations. The first step toward fluency in this somewhat difficult discipline is the playing of a strictly canonic duo at any interval and distance and in inversion at the octave, regardless of the immediate musical results.

Ex. II₉   (a) (Dux)

(Comes)

(b) Inversion at the octave
        (Comes)

(Dux)

(c) (Dux)

(Comes)

24

(d) Inversion at the octave

(Comes)

(Dux)

Upon attainment of a fair degree of dexterity through much practice, the student's senses will have been sharpened to the point where he will be able to avoid faulty voice leading. The somewhat unpolished appearance of the consecutive ninths and sevenths (Examples II_9a and II_9b) and the consecutive fifths and fourths (Examples II_9c and II_9d)[8] may be evaded by choosing a more appropriate point of entry for the *comes* (Example $II_{10}a$ and/or by melodic and rhythmic improvements of the lines. (Examle $II_{10}a$ and $II_{10}b$; play by sight inversions at the octave.)

Ex. II_{10} (a)

(b)

---

[8]For a more detailed discussion of conventional versus specifically contemporary treatment and related matters, see Chapter 6, "The Question of Idiom and Style."

9. In this context the pedal *cantus firmus*—frequently quoted in augmentation—should be practiced. The general approach to this very useful and adaptable mode of improvisation is by harmonizing given basses which, in augmentation, allow for considerable harmonic versatility. In preliminary exercises the student should familiarize himself with the practice of playing *cantus firmus* lines in the pedal while contenting himself with rather sketchy harmonizations in the manual (Example II₁₁).

The next step is the development of the manual texture to greater independence by introducing motivic elements and loosely knit imitation (Example II₁₂a).

26

A more advanced and perhaps slightly more difficult possibility is the application of trio technique: two mutually corresponding lines are played above the bass. These may be freely invented (Example II₁₂b) or related to the hymn (Example II₁₂c).

10. Sound cadential treatment produces structural clarity as well as convincing projection of extemporized musical thought. **Final cadences** and cadences concluding important sections within an improvisation should suggest a feeling of conclusion (see Examples II₁–II₃). A particularly worthwhile exercise is the adaptation of a previously introduced cadential formula to modulating or transposed phrases of related *cantus firmus* material. In Example II₁₃ such adaptations of given cadential formulas are demonstrated. Examples II₁b and II₁c are rendered as modulations to the dominant key. The *cantus firmus* remains literally identical, while the characteristic cadential lines have been so transposed as to confirm the modulation. This procedure is particularly successful in hymns, where the first phrase is repeated, as is the case in Walter's hymn. The student is urged to apply the same procedure to Examples II₂ and II₃ and to his own exercises.

It will be noted that measures 4 and 5 in Examples II₁₃a and II₁₃b create too strong a feeling of finality within the larger context of the hymn. Here is the place for the overlapping **inner cadence**. Examples II₁₃c and II₁₃d are simple applications of the principle of overlapping. The student must practice similar examples using deceptive cadential formulas (Examples II₁₄a and II₁₄b), suspensions (Example II₁₄c), alternate harmonizations (Example II₁₄d), or merely rhythmic motion (Example II₁₄e) to achieve the effect of continuity.

Ex. II₁₄ (a) ④ ⑤ (b) ④ ⑤ (c) ④ ⑤ (d) ④ ⑤ (e)

Finally, the technique of the "overlapping ending" for final cadence points should be practiced. Care must be taken to avoid banalities such as are shown in Example II₁₅a. Rather than tacking on such stereotyped progressions to the final chord, one should try to utilize material, derived perhaps from the last line of the hymn. It may be placed below the sustained final tonic (**melody point**, Example II₁₅b) or above it (**pedal point**, Example II₁₅c).

Ex. II₁₅ (a) (b) (c)

11. In addition to imaginative, imitative treatment of motivic material (Examples II₆, II₇, II₁₀, II₁₂, II₁₃, and II₁₅) the **sequence** must be noted as a useful—unfortunately frequently abused—and excellent means of achieving formal integration. When applied intelligently, it can serve effectively as a dramatic agent in interludes between quotations of the *cantus firmus* (Example II₁₆a). Its serviceability, particularly for purposes of modulation (Example II₁₆a) and enlivening static harmony (Example II₁₆b) must not be underestimated. Indiscriminate exploitation (Example II₁₆c) is, of course, undesirable. However, even slight deviations from literal quotations can result in sustained musical interest.

Ex. II$_{16}$ (a)

sequential interlude

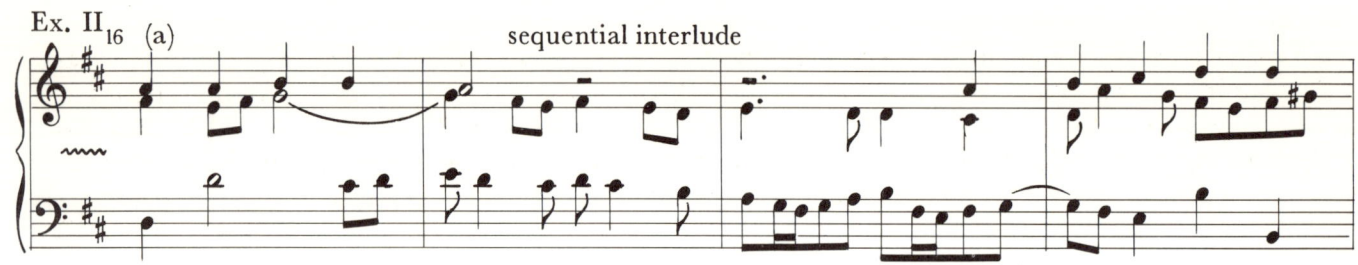

sequential remodulation

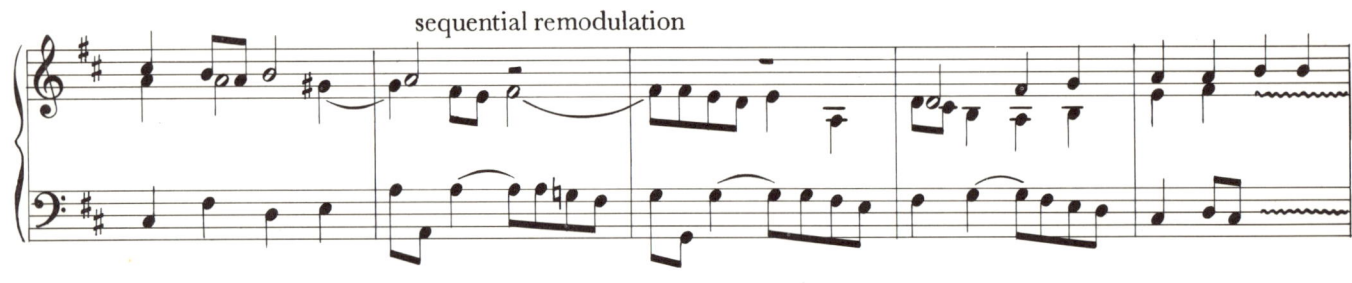

(b)

(c)

30

The foregoing points represent a survey of the most important basic features of the craft of improvisation. The student is urged to proceed to the following chapters only after a thorough study and an attainment of a degree of fluency in the skills discussed. Once again, it must be stressed that systematic practice will yield the desired results. The following suggestions for practice habits may be useful to the student.

STUDY AIDS

1. Place the **cantus firmus** line on music rack.

2. Think through entire improvisation in outline with particular attention to motivic features, number of measures (form), **bridges** and "seams" (to ensure polish and continuity), and mode of **cadence.**

3. Keep musical thoughts **simple enough** to **maintain complete control.** (Do not permit your fingers and feet to wander.)

4. At first, placing a sketchy outline on the music rack might be advisable. Caution: Do not condition yourself to depending on it.

5. If unable to remember entire phrases, try playing **individual parts separately,** then together in pairs and/or memorize by bars.

6. Always **transpose** exercises to various keys.

7. Try **singing** or humming individual parts while playing the remaining parts.

8. Most important of all, maintain **rhythmic continuity** even when practicing. Do not permit yourself any inconsistency in meter or rhythm. Mistakes or deviations from the mentally pre-planned outline are to be expected and must be smoothed out as casually as possible.

9. A very excellent aid in the study of improvisation is the tape recorder. Use it as often as possible in order to evaluate your own practice sessions.

Chapter 3

HYMN INTONATION

Characteristic features of improvisation are its defiance of permanent recording (except tape recording), its fleeting, transitory quality, and a degree of dependence on chance. These are its strongest assets and likewise its limitations. It should be remembered, however, that liturgical improvisation ought not to become a self-contained, independent entity. Instead it must be considered one of several interdependent approaches to creative musical expression.

Only the pedantic purist rejects the blending of several techniques *a priori*. The artist genuinely concerned with end results accepts "rules" governing technical aspects only insofar as they contribute to attaining his artistic objectives. The penciled study for a painting is in itself a legitimate artistic expression. The extent to which the creative will directs the lightly sketching fingers of the artist, and the extent to which his skilled fingers perform by habit, is an inscrutable part of the creative process. Suffice it to say that the painting was preceded and possibly strongly influenced by the sketch. But even if the sketch was never used for a painting, its disregard for detail in favor of evoking an incipient image is gratefully acknowledged by the eye.

Although musical improvisation may not precede composing a work of music, it is similar in some respects to pencil sketching. Its very nature forecloses structural intensity, a quality generally expected of notated compositions only. Yet, its lack of attention to detail can be its great asset because the encumbrance of musical notation is absent, permitting swift and direct—albeit sketchy—expression of musical thoughts. The extent to which the creative will is complemented at any given moment during an improvisation by "habitual" movement of the fingers remains unassessable. A certain amount of quasi-stereotyped, patterned "finger-composing" would seem to be inevitable; the ability to steer clear of clichés is perhaps one of the most difficult to attain. At any rate, one would always plan an improvisation carefully—just as one would any written composition. Of course, it cannot be preconceived in entirety, but its outline should be clearly established beforehand, even to the point of "sketching" a few motives on paper.

It is certain that many fine works for organ originated as improvisations.[9] Details, originally neglected, were supplied later by the composer in the process of notating and revising the improvisation. The sketch was transformed into a finished work of larger scope. Notwithstanding such transformation, such works frequently have a quality of freedom and casual lightness, indicating their mode of origin.

A far smaller number of works—particularly of pedagogical character or of stated practical intent—are undoubtedly improvisatory in character. One of the finest and most unique representatives of this latter group is a collection of chorale introductions by Johann Sebastian Bach's uncle, Johann Christoph.[10] The term "Präambulieren"—literally translated "preludize"—is strongly suggestive of improvisation within the practical framework of the worship service. The very brief but sound and intelligent hymn introductions confirm this suggestion.[11] The compositional technique used is simple and to the point. Above all, it satisfies the practical requirements of *brevity,* and *simplicity,* while clearly suggesting to the congregation *tune, tempo,* and *tonality.* These are the chief characteristics of the hymn intonation which is generally used for hymns other than the opening hymn and the hymn preceding the sermon. A very practical and easily adaptable type is discussed in the following section.

---

[9]See Appendix II-A, Selected Reference Material.

[10]Johann Christoph Bach, *44 Choräle zum Präambulieren*. Ed. Martin Fischer. Kassel: Bärenreiter, 1929.

[11]See also Fischer's lucid discussion: *Die organistische Improvisation im 17. Jahrhundert*. Kassel: Bärenreiter, 1929.

The Chorale Fughetta

It should be stressed that no strict, formal scheme is implied. The term alludes to a compositional technique, which avails itself of fugal patterns applied to material (usually the first line) of the hymn. A common form consists in two manual entries *(dux–comes)* followed by a pedal entry *(dux* or *comes)* which resorts at its earliest convenience to a pedal point on the dominant or tonic, above which the upper parts may form an extended coda, preferably by utilising hymn tune material (Example II₁₇b).

Hymn tune "Wir warten dein"

It will be noted that the *comes* has been introduced in the manner of a tonal answer in Example II₁₇b. This is not mandatory, as the degree of strict or free imitation may be determined by the organist. The possibilities for variants are legion, indeed. Example II₁₇c shows various forms of *comes* entries, while Example II₁₇d demonstrates a type of hymn intonation which makes use of imitation at any interval (in this case at the octave) rather than adhering to the fugal principle of tonic-dominant alternation by *dux* or *comes.*

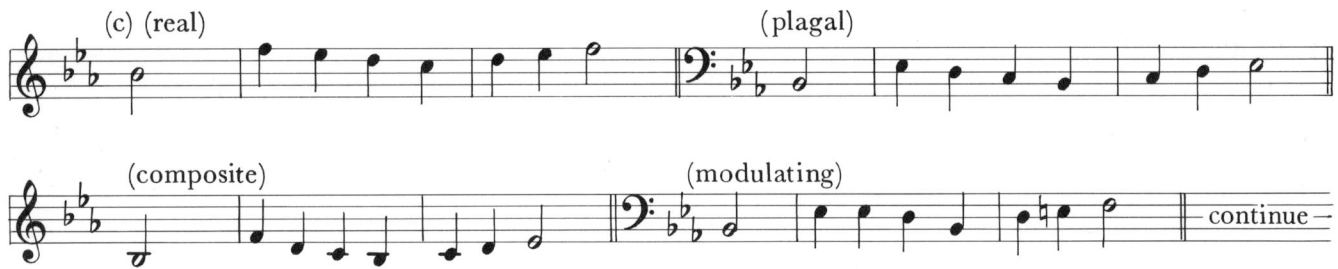

Example II₁₇e illustrates effective use of fillers for greater cadential impact.

As a means of enhancing the counterpoint, augmentation is introduced in Example II₁₈b in addition to strict imitation. This example exhibits a more contemporary texture, suggesting a moderate form of bitonality. The hymn (Example II₁₈a) is quoted in the version found in the Lutheran *Service Book and Hymnal* (1958).

Hymn tune "Wachet auf"

Ex. II₁₈ (a)

Hans Sachs (1513)
Philipp Nicolai (1599)

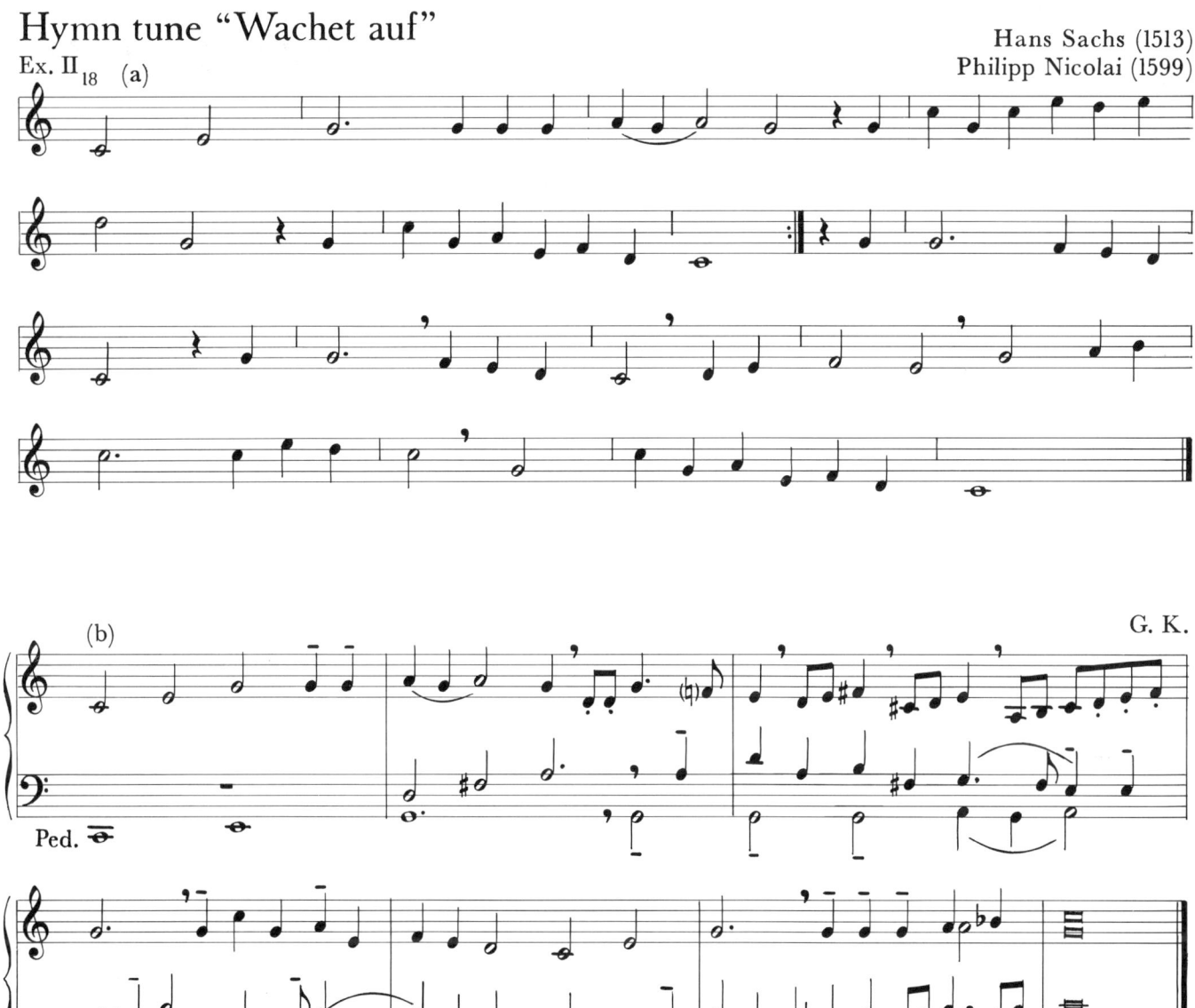

(b)

G. K.

Ped.

Mastery of such complex patterns can be achieved only through long-term practice as outlined above. Careful training in linear thinking and in playing melodically and rhythmically independent counterpoints to given *cantus firmi* in alternation between manuals and pedal will eventually be rewarded.

The even more complex and challenging technique of the chorale stretto[12] should be examined next. While it is not a frequently used technique of improvisation, it can be most effective and artistically satisfying. G. F. Kauffmann[13] supplies a practical and effective example of a chorale stretto *(totum in parte)* which could be improvisational in origin. As previously stated, the organist should not hesitate to rely on written clues, if they aid him in performing carefully planned textures. Ultimately it is of no interest whether an improvisation is performed with or without substantial aids in the form of notated "memos." The important feature is the quality of the music so performed.

---

[12]The classical example is J. S. Bach's *tour de force* in the final cadence of the fifth of his canonic variations on "Vom Himmel hoch" (BWV 769).

[13]Georg Friedrich Kauffmann. "Nun komm der Heiden Heiland D," *Harmonische Seelenlust* (1733). Ed. Pierre Pidoux. Kassel: Bärenreiter, 1951.

In Example II₁₉a five out of a total of seven *cantus firmus* lines are identified as components of the chorale stretto shown in Example II₁₉b. While a first glance at Example II₁₉b might be bewildering, closer examination does show a simple formal organization:

A and E form the pedal outline in augmentation.

B and D follow each other in the inner voices while C is superimposed, binding them together in the manner of a stretto. The upper voice provides much needed melodic freedom, while the inner voice sounds an augmented A above the pedal E.

With systematic approach and patient practice even such tricky patterns can be mastered.

Hymn tune "Herzliebster Jesu"

Johann Crüger (1640)

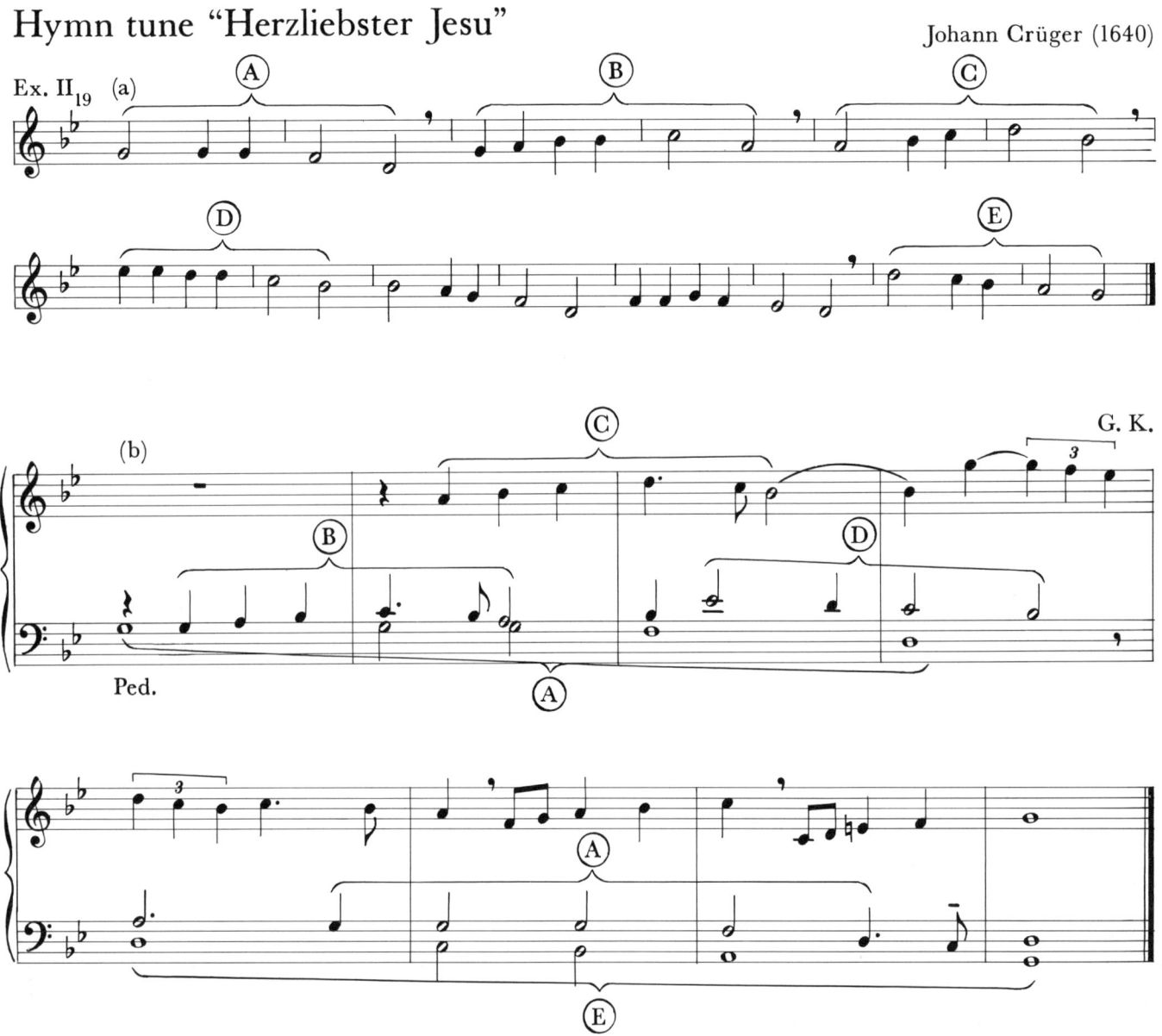

Finally, a type of intonation should be mentioned which employs the opposite procedure: relaxed contrapuntal treatment within a relatively homophonic texture. This treatment is suitable for hymn tunes which do not lend themselves well to contrapuntal treatment, or those which seem artificial and contrived when forcibly subjected to it. It is difficult to suggest any particular techniques for such hymn tunes. The organist's good taste and inventive resources must determine the particular handling of each case. While Example II₂₀b illustrates some undesirable features which should be avoided, Examples II₂₀c and II₂₀d suggest practical approaches for dignified and musically satisfactory results.

Hymn tune "Stephanos"

Ex. II₂₀ (a)

Henry W. Baker (1868)

37

Chapter 4

FREE ACCOMPANIMENT

One of the gratifying aspects of liturgical renewal within recent years is the emphasis on lively hymn singing. The inherently dramatic element in Christian hymnody—long obscured by a concept which equated piety with musical insipidity—has been rediscovered. The roles of congregation, choir, and organ (occasionally joined by instrumental groups) have been revitalized and reassigned. The use of *alternatim* practice—that is, the principle of alternating the rendition of individual hymn stanzas between congregation, choir, and organ—has resulted in a healthy striving for varied hymn accompaniments.[14] A number of excellent collections by various publishers provide fine opportunities for alert church musicians (see Appendix II-B). These settings range from simple accompaniments to complex arrangements. Instruments are frequently employed with the organ to good advantage.[15] The practicability of the *alternatim* usage and a growing availability of free accompaniments have facilitated widespread adoption.

Hymn Accompaniment: Congregational Stanza

The good organist will wish to accompany all congregational hymns in a lively and intelligent manner. He should vary his accompaniment from stanza to stanza in an effort to (a) underscore textual elements; (b) forestall congregational apathy caused by the exclusive use of one setting for all stanzas; and (c) induce a feeling of freshness and spontaneity.

A simple method for varying accompanimental textures is to render hymnal settings in a genuinely organistic manner patterned after Samuel Scheidt's great model.[16] In Example II₂₁b an unpretentious setting is shown which alters the hymnal version (Example II₂₁a, as quoted from *The Lutheran Hymnal* [1941]) only to the extent of introducing a few non-harmonic notes and mild metric and cadential modifications.

---

[14]Examples of sound application of *alternatim* usage to the liturgical year may be found in Ralph Gehrke's workbook, *Planning the Service*. St. Louis, Mo.: Concordia Publishing House, 1961.

[15]For an excellent collection of simple settings, see Willem Mudde, *Organ and Trumpet Accompaniments to Festival Hymns*. Minneapolis: Augsburg Publishing House, 1963.

[16]Most present-day hymnals exhibit note-by-note settings suitable for choral rendition; these are essentially descendent from Lucas Osiander's *Cantional* setting. With his *Fünfzig geistliche Lieder und Psalmen mit 4 Stimmen auf contrapunctweise also gesetzt, dass eine ganze christliche Gemein durchaus mitsingen kann* (1586), this imaginative theologian and musician created the **prototype of choral settings** designed to lead congregational hymn singing. (For quoted examples, see Arnold Schering, *Geschichte der Musik in Beispielen*. Wiesbaden: Breitkopf & Härtel, 1931, p. 142; and Konrad Ameln and Others, *Handbuch der deutschen evangelischen Kirchenmusik*, I:2 Göttingen: Vandenhoeck & Ruprecht, 1942; pp. 132, 149, 202.) Scheidt's *Görlitzer Tabulaturbuch* (1650) (see Christhard Mahrenholz, ed. New York: C. F. Peters, Preface 1940) supplies the **prototype of organ settings** designed for congregational accompaniment. It is this author's fond hope that future hymnals be issued in separate editions for congregation (melody edition), choir (choral settings), and organist (two, three, and four part organ settings).

Hymn tune "Nicaea"

Ex. II₂₁ (a)

John B. Dykes 1861

Setting, G. K.

39

This approach makes conscious use of the harmonization found in the hymnal. It is the simplest form of varied hymn accompaniment. With a sufficient amount of practice the student will be able to develop this technique to a degree of independence. In Example II$_{21}$c the harmonic outlines of the hymnal setting are only loosely preserved. Cadential and metric modifications are carried to greater length. The degree of variance has been increased.

Setting, G. K.

Having gained versatility in paraphrasing the hymnal settings, the student must now proceed to improvise his own accompaniments. (Place the hymn melody on the music rack!) Example II$_{21}$d shows a two-part improvisation in which the *cantus firmus* is given to the left hand (possibly with reed chorus 16′ 8′ 4′ and light mixture) while the right hand (Prinzipals 8′ 4′ 2′ and mixture) plays a freely roving counterpoint consisting of easily adaptable fanfare motives. Example II$_{21}$e is a three-part manual improvisation in a more contemporary idiom.

Setting, G. K.

Setting, G. K.

41

It is virtually impossible to point out the many possibilities for varied hymn accompaniments. In addition to varied harmonic treatment of each stanza, manual changes and subtly altered registrations enliven congregational hymn singing. A note of caution, however, must be sounded against overdoing organ accompaniments.[17] The good organist will always strive to maintain musical rapport with the congregation. It is not possible to prescribe binding rules or to formulate a neat set of universally applicable instructions. Intuitive awareness of the congregation's rhythmic pulse and sensitive divination of the narrow borderline between the "acceptable" and the "offensive" in any given situation are decisive factors. A carefully planned program of gradually conditioning the congregation to a variety of possibilities will insure positive and consistent congregational response.

Organ Chorale: *Alternatim* Stanza

Antiphonal rendition in the widest sense[18] is an excellent and highly recommendable practice; it is specifically useful for festival hymns, for the hymn of the week (month), for the hymn(s) sung during the distribution of the elements of Holy Communion, for opening (processional) hymns in such special services as Confirmation, Ordination, and Thanksgiving, and for dedicatory, commemorative, and other special occasions. Ideally, at least one hymn should be rendered antiphonally in every service. The organ stanza (*versette*) serves in an important capacity. While members of the congregation and choir read the *text* of the particular stanza to themselves, the organ renders its *melody* by way of an organ chorale. Whenever possible, additional forces may be used. The possibilities for alternatim practice are virtually inexhaustible.[19] The organ stanza may be fairly elaborate, although it is generally agreed that it should not exceed the formal limitation of the organ chorale, *i.e.*, it should quote the *cantus firmus* in its entirety and usually without any interludes between *cantus firmus* phrases.[20] In Example II[22] the *cantus firmus* is assigned to the pedal (16′) in augmentation, the manual parts are playable on one or two manuals. The tempo remains that of the congregational hymn ($\bigl.\downarrow = \downarrow\bigr.$).

---

[17]In the author's opinion, organ modulations between successive congregational stanzas for the mere sake of color lack functional purpose. Frequently they strain the congregation's unison range. Although such modulatory interludes may be handled well on the organ, they constitute needless complications for the average congregation.

[18]Creative application of alternatim practice to any number of available performance groups can result in very satisfactory *concertato* formations. Accompanied singly and *tutti* by choir, organ, and/or instrumental groups, congregational stanzas alternate with stanzas rendered individually or in ensemble combinations by these accompanying forces. Such choral or instrumental solo renditions may be fairly elaborate. Key changes may be necessitated by considerations of ranges of the performing group or soloist. The most effective result is obtained when the *alternatim* group or soloist proceeds directly into the related key without modulatory interlude. This may be done whenever the key relationship is from the tonic to dominant, subdominant, mediant or submediant. The return to the tonic for the following congregational stanza may well create a pleasant *rondeau* effect. For more distant keys, transitional modulations and remodulations are recommended. Care should be taken to indicate clearly in the bulletin the intended sequence of alternation.

[19]Although this book deals with the mechanics of organ improvisation only, a few collections suitable for effective *alternatim* usage are given here for the benefit of the church musician in search of widely useful materials.

Georg Friedrich Kauffmann. *Six Chorales for Organ and Oboe or Trumpet* from *Harmonische Seelenlust*. Ed. Richard T. Gore. St. Louis, Mo.: Concordia Publishing House, 1956.

Johannes H. Koch. *Five Intradas and Chorales on Easter Hymns: Organ and Trumpet*. St. Louis, Mo.: Concordia Publishing House, 1963.

Gerhard Krapf. *Chorale Intradas for Brass Choir*. 2 vols. St. Louis, Mo.: Concordia Publishing House, 1963.

Johann Ludwig Krebs. *Eight Chorale Preludes for Organ with Trumpet (or Oboe)*. Ed. E. Power Biggs. New York: Mercury Music Corp., 1947.

Harald Rohlig. *Intradas and Chorales: Organ and Trumpet*. St. Louis, Mo.: Concordia Publishing House, 1959.

[20]The most artistic and advanced examples of this type of chorale elaboration are found in Bach's *Orgelbüchlein*. Pachelbel's *cantus firmus* settings found in his *Chorale Partitas*, *op. cit.*, are less demanding but practical models of high quality.

Ex. II$_{22}$ (For hymn tune see Ex. II$_{17}$ a) G. K.

c.f. (16')

Often the organist will wish to keep the *cantus firmus* of the organ stanza rhythmically identical with the congregational stanzas for the sake of dramatic drive. Frequently he may not have enough time to change to elaborate *cantus firmus* registrations (unless the a cappella choir or instrumental group[s] relieve[s] him of congregational accompaniment during the stanza immediately preceding the organ chorale). He may also have to provide a free accompaniment for a choral unison stanza. In this case he would be expected to render a setting more elaborate in harmony and counterpoint while quoting the hymn *cantus firmus* literally. This may also apply to congregational singing of well-known hymns. Examples II$_{23}$a, II$_{23}$b, II$_{24}$a, and II$_{24}$b illustrate such contingencies in a moderately contemporary idiom.

(For hymn tune see Ex. II$_{18}$a)

Ex. II$_{23}$ (a) Three-part setting   Setting, G. K.

(b) Four-part setting, also usable
as c.f. setting

Setting, G. K.

45

(For hymn tune see Ex. II$_{19}$ a)

Ex. II$_{24}$ (a) Three-part setting

Setting, G. K.

(b) Four-part setting

Setting, G. K.

Finally, the jointly rendered hymn improvisation should be noted as an excellent means of combining solo instruments or unison voices for festive occasions. Again, the quotation of the *cantus firmus* by melody instruments or unison voices is literal, while a freely imitative accompaniment provides variety. (Example II₂₅).

Hymn tune "Allein Gott in der Höh"

Nicolaus Decius (1539)
Setting, G.K.

Ex. II₂₅

47

While an exhaustive survey of the infinite possible uses of the organ chorale has not been attempted, it is hoped that the outline of basic procedures given here will stimulate the student to practice organ improvisation intelligently and creatively. Obviously, the well-improvised organ chorale need not be confined to the liturgical functions of congregational or choral accompaniment only, but may serve also as chorale prelude, voluntary, or organ meditation during the offering, Holy Communion, and similar occasions.

Chapter 5

HYMN PRELUDE

[Note: Supplementary exercises to various types of hymn elaboration discussed in this chapter may be found in Appendix III, page 101.]

Cantus firmus Treatment

One of the simplest types of hymn elaboration is the organ chorale, enlarged by short interludes between the individual *cantus firmus* lines and frequently—although not always—by a short introductory statement.[21] These interludes need not be derived from the hymn. Imitation may be rather free, although a certain amount of motivic correspondence is desirable. The main function of the interludes is to provide smooth harmonic transitions between the individual *cantus firmus* lines. In Example II₂₆b such a simple hymn elaboration is shown. The only element of motivic correspondence is the chromatically descending and ascending line. Although the interludes in this example are exactly two bars in duration, there is no need to keep them identical. Indeed, interludes of different length are quite effective. Note also the good effect of dissonant *cantus firmus* entries.

Hymn tune "Hamburg"

Ex. II₂₆   (a)

adapted by Lowell Mason (1824)

(b) **Pensively, not fast** (♩ = 69)   G.K.

---

[21]For a typical example, see G. F. Kauffmann, "Lobt Gott, ihr Christen, allzugleich A," *Harmonische Seelenlust, op. cit.*

Such simple hymn preludes must be practiced systematically by the student. The *cantus firmus* should also be assigned to inner and bass voices in the left hand, and to the pedal on 16′ (bass), 8′ (tenor or alto), and 4′ (descant) basis (see Examples II₃ and II₄).

In Example II₂₇ the same type of hymn prelude is demonstrated with ornate rather than literal *cantus firmus* quotation (see Example II₂a). Obviously, such elaborate *cantus firmus* versions are impractical for rendition on the pedals. While occasionally occuring in the left hand as tenor or alto, they are most frequently assigned to the right hand.[22] The interludes between the individual *cantus firmus* lines have been rendered as one phrase. The left-hand part is organized into two corresponding five-bar phrases, of which the second represents a variant of the first. After a brief interlude the same phrase is reintroduced in the form of another variant (measures 14-18). The pedal is used in the manner of pedal points on the tonic at the beginning and end of the improvisation, interrupted by a descending figure (measures 5-7 and 10-14) which is reminiscent of the last *cantus firmus* line.

---

[22]A fine example is "O Herre Gott, dein göttlich Wort A" in G. F. Kauffmann's *Harmonische Seelenlust, op. cit.*

(For hymn tune see Ex. II₁₉ a)

Ex. II₂₇ **Gently, slow quarters** (♩ = 58)

c.f.

G.K.

Organ

II Gentle reed 8'
Zimbel II

III Ged. 8'
Rohrfl. 4'

Pedal

Bordun 16'
Flute 8'

51

Frequently, the interludes between *cantus firmus* lines are derived from common motivic material, which may be free or related to the hymn. This device is useful for achieving structural uniformity. Examples II$_{28}$b and II$_{28}$d show hymn preludes of this type.[23]

Hymn tune "O Jesu Christ, meins Lebens Licht"

Ex. II$_{28}$ (a)   Nürnberg Gesangbuch (1676)

Flessibile ($\quad$ = 76)

(b)   G. K.

c.f. (16')

---

[23]See also Friedrich Wilhelm Zachow, "Erbarm dich mein, o Herre Gott," *Gesammelte Werke, op. cit.*

Hymn tune "Freu dich sehr, o meine Seele"

Louis Bourgeois (1551)

Johann Gottfried Walther

taken from: Johann Gottfried Walther, *Gesammelte Werke für Orgel*. Ed. Max Seiffert. *Denkmäler Deutscher Tonkunst, XXVI*. Wiesbaden: Breitkopf & Härtel, copyright 1958. Reprinted by permission.

Ostinato Patterns, Hymn Passacaglia, Use of Drones.

Ostinato patterns are easily adaptable to improvisation. The wealth of possibilities defies enumeration, although some typical ones may be cited. The *ostinato* motive may be confined to one part—frequently the bass—or it may form a solid pattern together with the accompanimental parts. It may remain static throughout, or it may be transposed successively. It may be derived from the hymn or consist of contrasting material.[24] Example II₂₉b shows an improvisation which uses a double *ostinato*. Superimposed on the regularly recurring three-bar pedal *ostinato* is a six-bar left-hand phrase, which appears three times. This pattern is interrupted by three bars (measures 13-15) between the second and third occurrence of the manual phrase. As an optional feature, a melody instrument may be added, forming a canon at the octave with the right-hand *cantus firmus*. The role of this instrument regarding *comes* entries and *cantus firmus* alterations should be discussed prior to performance, or a written part may be provided (Example II₂₉a, b).

Hymn tune "Es ist ein Ros"

Ex. II₂₉ (a)   16th century

---

[24]For effective use of *ostinato* patterns, see Helmut Walcha, "Herzliebster Jesu, was hast du verbrochen," in *Fünfundzwanzig Choralvorspiele für Orgel*, Frankfurt: C. F. Peters, 1954; and "Gottes Sohn ist kommen," and "O Mensch, bewein dein Sünde gross," in *Choralvorspiele für Orgel*, Frankfurt: Henry Litolff's Verlag, 1963.

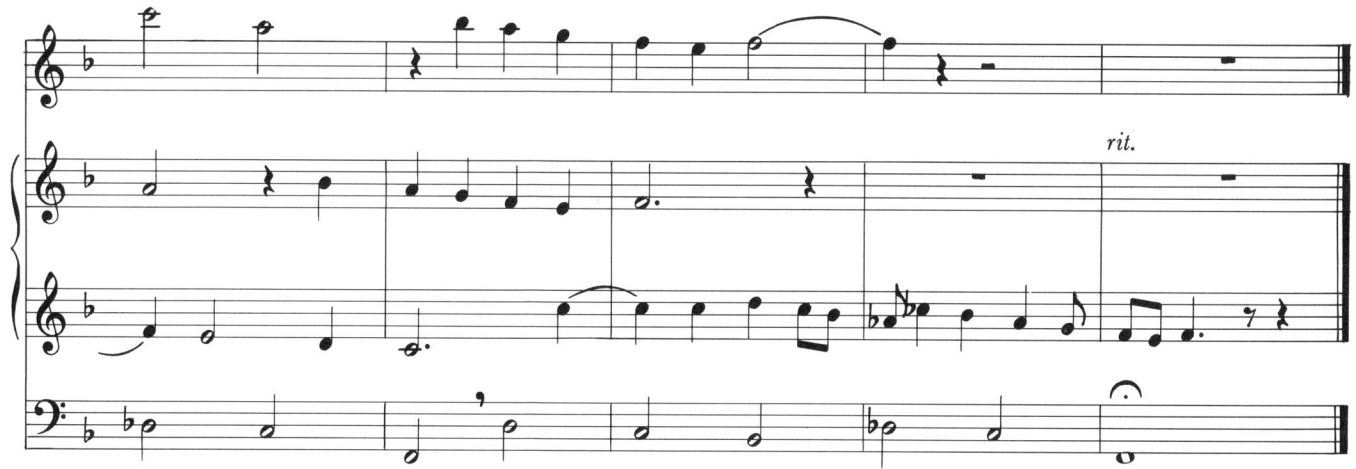

In Example II30 the same formal plan is used in a version for harpsichord (pianoforte) and violin. It is conceivable that Christmas music of this nature might be requested on short notice, for instance for use within the context of a liturgical play or a similar situation.

Ex. II_{30} G. K.

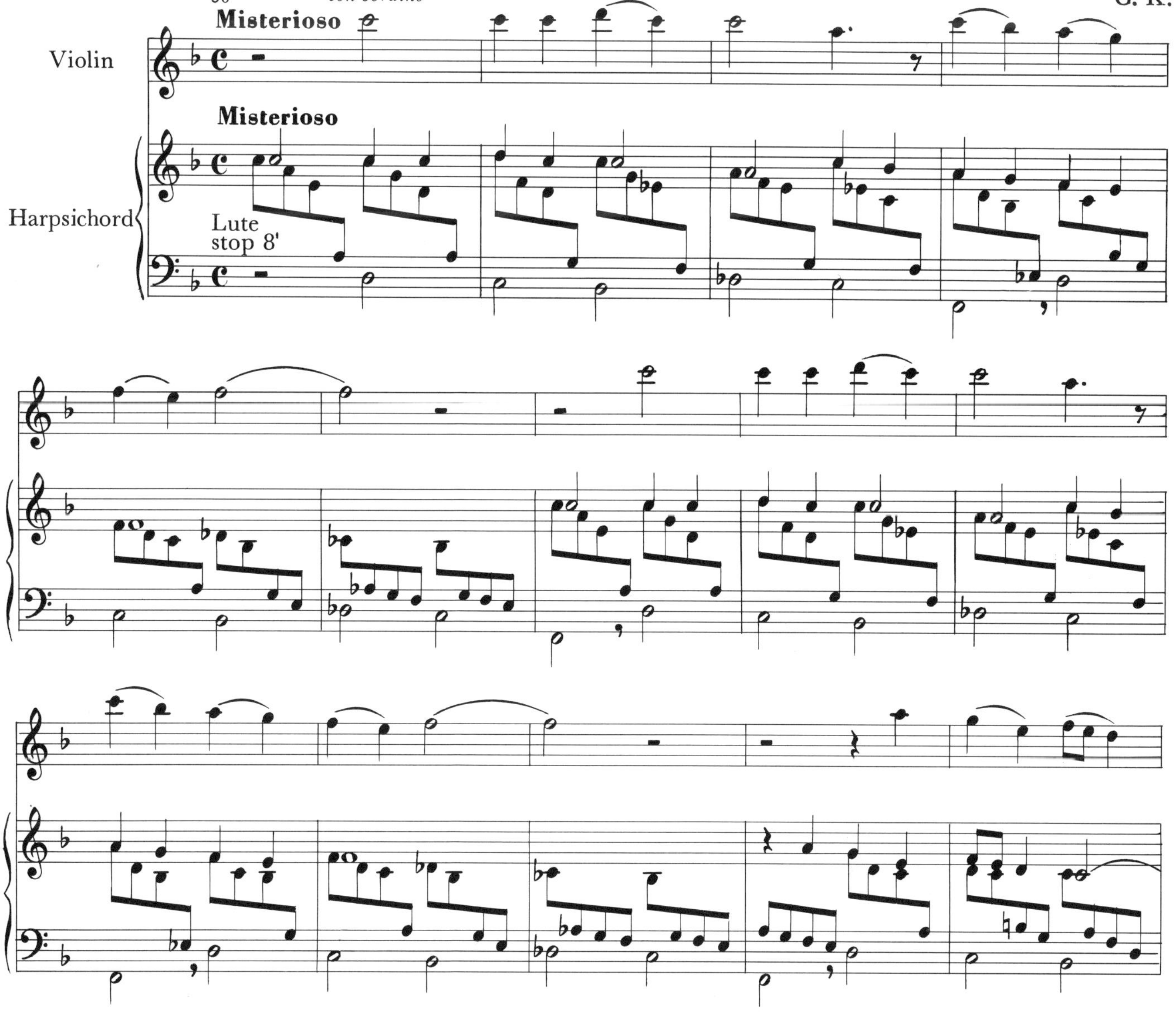

The hymn passacaglia[25] is based on a pedal *ostinato* which is derived from the hymn. In successive variations above this ground the *cantus firmus* is introduced, line by line. The *ostinato* may be transposed and/or switched to the manuals for purposes of modulations and for the sake of color and musical interest. Examples II₃₁b and II₃₁d show short improvisations in the manner of such a hymn passacaglia. Larger improvisations might be organized sectionally, each section introducing several variations on *cantus firmus* lines.

Hymn tune "Aus meines Herzens Grunde"

Ex. II₃₁ (a)

Hamburg (1598)

---

[25]See also Vincent Lübeck, "Zugabe: Lobt Gott, ihr Christen allzugleich," *Klavier-Übung* (1728). Ed. Hilmar Trede. New York: C. F. Peters, 1941.

Forthrightly ($\quad$ = 135)

G.K.

59

Hymn tune "Wer nur den lieben Gott lässt walten"

Georg Neumark (1657)

Kleine Passacaglia

Johann Nepomuk David

(d) Ruhig und gesangvoll

16' + 8'

nur 8'

+ 4'

60

+ 4'

4' + Man.-Koppel

II

Bewegt

mf

zarte Zungen an

61

taken from: Johann Nepomuk David, *Choralwerk, II.* Wiesbaden: Breitkopf & Härtel, copyright 1932/1960. Reprinted by permission.

An effective device is the use of pedal points on the tonic (sometimes also on the dominant) in the manner of drones. Together with the characteristic 6/8 meter and light flute registration, such drones produce charming pastorale effects, particularly suitable for Christmas hymns. Example II$_{32}$b shows such a hymn improvisation.[26] In example II$_{32}$d, a gently pulsating tonic pedal point is temporarily shifted to the mediant key.

Hymn tune "Wir Christenleut han jetzund Freud" or "O Jesu Christ, dein Kripplein ist"

Johann Crüger (1653)

Ex. II$_{32}$ (a)

---

[26]For another typical example see Helmut Walcha's "Den die Hirten lobten sehre," *Fünfundzwanzig Choralvorspiele, op. cit.*

Hymn tune "Es kommt ein Schiff geladen"

Cologne (1608)

Sostenuto

Ernst Pepping

taken from: Ernst Pepping, *Kleines Orgelbuch*. Mainz: B. Schott, copyright 1941. Reprinted by permission.

The *ritornello* is easily adaptable to chorale improvisations. It serves as introduction and coda respectively and as contrast between *cantus firmus* sections. Frequently an extended phrase (its motivic material) is often—although not always—free, that is, not hymn-derived. It may be transposed to obtain harmonic color, or in order to accommodate varying tonalities of the *cantus firmus* lines.[27] (See Example II33.)

Hymn tune "Stuttgart"

[27]An excellent example is Paul Manz's "All Glory Be to God on High," *Ten Chorale Improvisations, op.* 5, Set I. St. Louis, Mo.: Concordia Publishing House, 1962.

The *bicinium*[28] employs two parts only, one which renders the *cantus firmus,* while the other—usually the left hand—supplies chorale-related interludes. These frequently take the form of *ritornelli* (Example II$_{34}$b) or show preimitation (Examples II$_{35}$b and II$_{35}$d). Example II$_{34}$b is essentially a *bicinium,* even though occasional fillers have been added for harmonic color.

Hymn tune "Warum sollt ich mich denn grämen"

J. G. Ebeling (1666)

Ex. II$_{34}$ (a)

[28]See J. S. Bach's "Allein Gott in der Höh," (BWV 711); preimitation is used by G. F. Kauffmann in Example II$_{35}$d "Christus, der uns selig macht," *Harmonische Seelenlust, op. cit.* Further examples may be found in Scheidt's *Tabulatura Nova,* III. Ed. Christhard Mahrenholz. Hamburg: Ugrino Verlag, 1928.

Flessibile ($\quarternote = 96$)

(b)   Slender Plenum Registration

G.K.

67

Hymn tune "Hyfrydol"

Ex. II₃₅ (a)

Rowland H. Prichard (1855)

senza rit.

Deciso (♩ = 116)

(b)

c.f.

G.K.

(Ob. werk)

(Pos.) *f*

poco a poco rit.

69

Hymn tune "Christus, der uns selig macht"

14th century

(c)

Georg Friedrich Kauffmann

(d)

c.f.

70

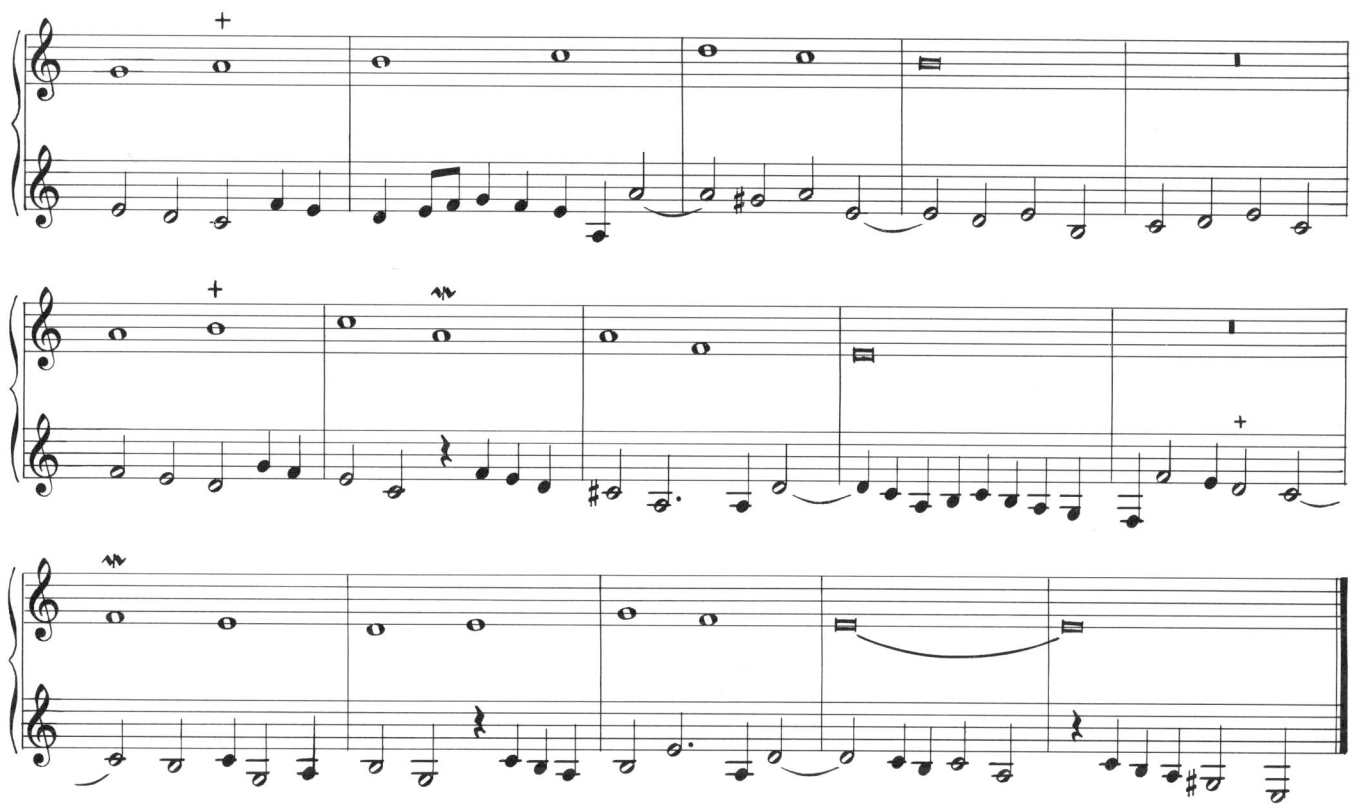

taken from: Georg Friedrich Kauffmann, *Harmonische Seelenlust* (1733). Ed. Pierre Pidoux. Kassel: Bärenreiter, copyright 1951. Reprinted by permission.

Canonic Treatment

Even though canonic formations[29] are not as readily adaptable to improvisation as some of the other modes of hymn elaboration, careful planning and intense concentration will eventually lead to mastery. The use of canons at the octave is recommended as the most practical type for improvisation. In Example II36b the *cantus firmus* is introduced as a canon at the octave. For interest's sake the *dux* switches to the upper voice in the third *cantus firmus* line, returning to the middle part for the final cadence.

Careful consideration must be given to preplanning the canon. Not every hymn tune can be fitted naturally into canonic patterns. The non-canonic part(s) must be so designed as to complement rhythmically, melodically, and harmonically the skeletal outline furnished by the canonic parts.

Hymn tune "Dundee" (French)

Ex. II₃₆ (a)   Scottish Psalter (1615)

---

[29]For unsurpassed models see Bach's canonic variations on "Vom Himmel hoch" (BWV 769); and from his *Orgelbüchlein:* "Christe, du Lamm Gottes," "Christus, der uns selig macht," "Erschienen ist der herrlich Tag," "Gott durch deine Güte," "Hilf Gott, dass mir's gelinge," "In dulci jubilo," "Liebster Jesu, wir sind hier," and "O Lamm Gottes, unschuldig."

In moderate tempo (♩ = 76)

G. K.

(b)

Pos: Fl. 8' 4'

c.f.

Ob. werk: Krummhorn 8'

c.f.

Subbass 16' Pommer 8'

Pos.

Ob. werk

Ob. werk

Pos.

(b)

Pos.

Ob. werk

In Example II₃₇b the upper parts form a canon at the octave, melodically derived from the *cantus firmus*, which is played in the pedal on 16′ foundation (note suggested registration). In bar 19, the distance between the two canonic voices has been reduced from four beats to two for increased intensity.

Hymn tune "Morgenglanz der Ewigkeit"

Ex. II₃₇ (a)   Freylinghausen's Gesangbuch, (1704)

Gently flowing (♩ = 69)   G. K.

(b)

One or two manuals Flutes 8′ 4′ Zimbel

Pedal Subbass 16′ Bauernflöte 2′

c.f.

73

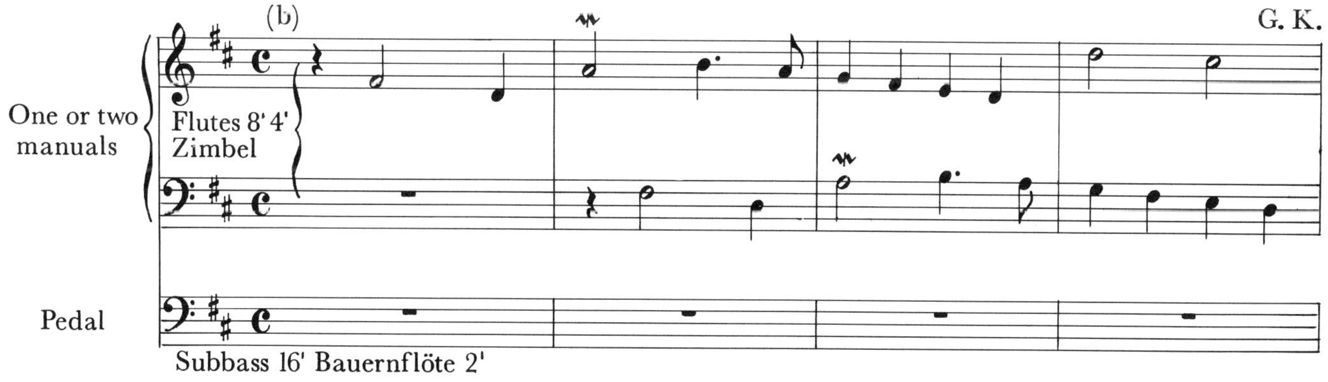

Both examples are simple in concept. Canons at the fifth or at other intervals should be attempted only on the basis of considerable experience and with the benefit of highly developed skill. In any case, the borderline between improvisation and notated composition is approached the more closely as canonic patterns increase in complexity.

Chorale Fugue

The technique of the chorale fugue consists in fugal preimitation. Individual *cantus firmus* lines are utilized as fugal subjects and precede the quotation of each *cantus firmus* line in the form of fugue expositions. The first of these expositions is usually complete and frequently rather extended. The succeeding expositions are often incomplete.[30] Example II38b illustrates a plausibly simple adaptation of the chorale fugue to improvisation. The hymn tune (Example II38a) is quoted in the version appearing in the Lutheran *Service Book and Hymnal* (1958).

Hymn tune "Gott des Himmels"

Ex. II38 (a)

Heinrich Albert (1642)

Brightly flowing (♩ = 112)

(b)

G. K.

Gt. *f*

16' 8' 4' reeds

---

[30]For an excellent example, see Johann Pachelbel, "Allein Gott in der Höh sei Ehr, 6b," *Ausgewählte Orgelwerke*, II, *op. cit.* "O Mensch bewein dein Sünde gross," *ibid.*, shows a more relaxed approach; excepting the first exposition, imitation at the octave rather than strict *dux-comes* alternation is used throughout.

Ornate, Embellished *Cantus firmus*

Ornate *cantus firmus* treatment with free accompaniment has been illustrated previously (see Example II$_{27}$). In Example II$_{39}$, a freely embellished *cantus firmus* is superimposed onto a scheme of preimitation very much akin to the chorale fugue.[31] The imitation within the interludes, however, is more relaxed.

---

[31]See also J. G. Walther, "Es ist das Heil uns kommen her," *op. cit.*

In Example II$_{40}$b a very free hymn elaboration is shown. The *cantus firmus* is presented in an ornate form, which is predominantly isometric. The accent lies on melodic and harmonic color, rather than strict contrapuntal techniques.[32] This type of improvisation is particularly effective as *versette* played in *alternatim* style with choir or congregation. Obviously, recognition of highly ornate *cantus firmi* by the congregation cannot be expected. This technique should, therefore, be reserved for independent organistic functions within the service.

---

[32]See G. F. Kauffmann's "Nun danket alle Gott, B Alio modo," *op. cit.*

Hymn tune "Die güldne Sonne"

Ex. II$_{40}$ (a)

Johann Georg Ebeling (1666)

Brightly flowing (♩. = 96)

(b) *sempre leggiero*

On one
or two
manuals

subito rit.

Echo Hymn

The echo hymn[33] is very easily adapted to improvisation. It consists in colorful harmonization of the hymn tune, interspersed between the *cantus firmus* phrases of which are "echo" fragments which are harmonized differently and played with contrasting registration. This is a technique developed during the nineteenth century and is particularly useful for hymn tunes dating from that period, although it can also be applied effectively to chorale tunes.[34] The *cantus firmus* is frequently subjected to slight alterations due to the elaborate harmonic rhythm. (See Example II₄₁b.)

---

[33]The term "echo hymn" was coined for lack of a commonly accepted usage.

[34]For various applications of this technique see Max Reger, "Seelenbräutigam," *Orgelwerke, op. 67: Zweiundfünfzig leicht ausführbare Vorspiele zu den gebräuchlichsten evangelischen Chorälen*, III. Berlin: Bote & Bock, 1903.

Johannes Brahms, "11. O Welt, ich muss dich lassen," *Sämtliche Werke, Ausgabe der Gesellschaft der Musikfreunde in Wien*, XVI. Wiesbaden: Breitkopf & Härtel, 1927.

Anton Wilhelm Leupold, "O Lamm Gottes unschuldig," "Christ ist erstanden," *Orgelbuch*. Ed. Ulrich Leupold. Berlin: Verlag Merseburger, ed. 828 (selected reprint of *Orgelbuch*, 4 vols. Wolfenbüttel: Georg Kallmeyer Verlag, 1933).

Composite Forms

The foregoing discussion is an attempt to describe certain types of chorale elaborations that are adaptable to improvisation. However, it should be remembered that such a typological organization is feasible only for the didactic purpose of establishing illustrative models. None of the formal schemes discussed should be considered as unalterable and inflexible molds. Rather, each one represents a prototypal approach to practical organistic usage. The invention of specific thematic material, the choice of contrapuntal patterns, harmonic motion, rhythmic considerations, and such practical aspects as duration and general musical character contribute in large measure to the specific structural organization of any chorale elaboration.

Furthermore, it must be understood that formal elements of any one of several types discussed may be used simultaneously or successively within a given chorale elaboration. To attempt an enumeration of the manifold possibilities open to the composer and/or improviser would be a task too far-reaching for the scope of this book. Example II$_{42}$ may speak for itself as an illustration of freely applied usage of compositional patterns that have been discussed in this chapter.

Fantasia

(For Hymn tune see Ex. II$_1$)

Ex. II$_{42}$ **Deciso** ($\quad$+-112) With strong plenum registration

Chapter 6

THE QUESTION OF IDIOM AND STYLE

It would be a momentous task—and one that would exceed the scope of this book—to assemble, organize, and analyze systematically the many divergent schools of thought, style elements, concepts, and patterns of musical composition that have come to the fore during the past two decades. Not only have the technical aspects of handling tonal and sound materials and those of melodic, harmonic, rhythmic, metric, and formal organization been subjected to a number of changes; but also the artistic and creative philosophies have undergone far-reaching reinterpretations and often have produced widely differing views—frequently verbalized in very articulate manner by the composers themselves. For example, Stravinsky still thinks of music as "a form of communion with our fellow man—and with the Supreme Being,"[35] whereas some avant garde composers of the sixties have stated in varying degrees of emphasis that communication [let alone communion] is not their primary objective.

A prodigious number of new systems of musical expression are constantly developing, some of which are radical, while others derive from conservative sources. Since 1923 when Schönberg wrote his *Ten Piano Pieces, op.* 23, we have witnessed the evolution of twelve-tone composing, its transformation to post-war serialism, and the emergence of electronic music with its many, as yet unrealized, possibilities, as well as a broad current of modified traditionalism.

With the exception of a few isolated works,[36] organ composing has remained within this traditionalist stream, thus lagging considerably behind some contemporary developments. This is true of recital literature as well as of service music. Rather than engaging in philosophic speculations concerning this apparent deficiency,[37] it might be helpful to point out some very practical reasons:

1. The complexities of sound and color resources of the organ require a careful study on the part of the composer wishing to exploit functionally the instrument's possibilities.[38]

2. The contemporary composer, accustomed to thinking in terms of specific sounds and extraordinary color combinations attainable through imaginative orchestration, sees himself reduced to having to entrust the finer points of color and dynamics to the organist. At best, he can indicate the pitch level and stop family (flutes 8', 4'; no mixtures, *etc.*), hoping that the organist will translate such general directions into the specific possibilities available to him at his particular instrument. Good writing for organ presupposes **latitude** of color concepts. Ideally, organ compositions should offer various alternatives for color realization.

3. The organ is singularly resistant to unconventional special sound effects for which contemporary composers have shown marked interest (flutter tongue, tapping woodwind keys without blowing, *scordatura*, and various means of preparing the pianoforte).

4. The rigidity and dynamic inflexibility of organ sound and the instrument's predisposition for linear textures constitute a substantial obstacle for the composer whose artistic and creative instincts are directed toward the opposite concept of highly refined color distinctions, subtle dynamic shadings and polyphonic textures of a less ponderous nature.

---

[35]Igor Stravinsky, *Poetics of Music,* trans. Arthur Knodel and Ingolf Dahl. Cambridge: Harvard University Press, 1947, p. 142.

[36]Individualistic recent examples which exhibit uncompromising organ textures are: James H. Case, *Sonnet.* New York: H. W. Gray, 1964. William Hibbard, *Fantasy for Organ, Trumpet, Trombone and Percussion* (available from composer, 1965). Vincent Persichetti, *Shima B'koli.* Philadelphia: Elkan-Vogel, 1963.

[37]In this regard, see Gerhard Krapf, "Concerning Composition for the Organ," *Response* VI/2 (1964). Reprinted *Amer. Guild of Organists Quarterly* X/1 (1965).

[38]Berlioz may have overstated the problem but nevertheless has recognized its importance by saying ". . . no composer, in our opinion, can understand [the resources of the instrument and their application] adequately unless he himself is an accomplished organist." Hector Berlioz, *Treatise on Instrumentation,* rev. Richard Strauss, trans. Theodore Front. New York: Edwin F. Kalmus, 1948, p. 246.

5. The *plenum* ensemble qualities of the organ with their built-in series of harmonics constitute a disturbing challenge to the contemporary composer's discriminating sense of pitch relationships. Often he is apt to reject precisely those aspects of organ sound which are essential to the nature of the instrument.

The conservative qualities of contemporary organ music—particularly of liturgical organ music—are directly related to these phenomena. An attendant result has been the growing estrangement between sacred and secular music, particularly apparent in organ literature. With the exception of Messiaen, no composer-organist has attained a status of importance outside of church musical circles within recent years.[39] Perhaps this reflects a certain amount of mutual indifference by church musician and secular composer alike, which is all too frequently explained by the covenient reference to the growing rift between contemporary musical thought and liturgical usage. The reality of this rift, however, should be a source of concern to church musicians, not because of the implied inferior status of church music, but because of the dangers of inbreeding inherent in isolation. One basic but all-important step toward improving the situation would be to correct the mistaken notion according to which any one style or idiom is "suitable" or "unsuitable" by virtue of a code of esthetic rules set down by some committee. An equally important step would be recognition of the need for professional excellence of church music staffs, for salary schedules commensurate with their training, and adequate provisions for continued professional training. This basic need for broadening horizons in the field of church music cannot be overstressed.[40]

✧   ✧   ✧

Having examined some of the problems facing the contemporary composer with regard to the organ, we must now consider some practical aspects of organ music for the service with special attention to improvising hymn elaborations.

One of the first points of order is to recognize the liturgical function of organ music—both free and chorale-based. This in itself clearly implies *communication* as a primary objective. It necessitates a mode of musical expression calculated to communicate to a maximum number of listeners without any loss of musical excellence.[41] In short, a composer-organist must be willing to work within a clearly defined liturgical framework and to align his creative powers with the objective of the widest possible comprehensibility.[42]

The second prerequisite is the composer's willingness to recognize, accept, and exploit fully the idiosyncracies as well as the limitations of the organ. Fortunately, we are in a position to profit from the wealth of knowledge and practical insights gained during the past decades, thanks to the international organ movement *(Orgelbewegung)*. We have learned that any attempt to alter, bypass, or ignore the instrument's distinctive and peculiar qualities—either by means of abnormal organ design or by unidiomatic writing—will only yield musically unsatisfactory and quite artificial results. Rather than searching for fringe effects, the contemporary composer must acquaint himself thoroughly with all aspects of organ techniques. By shaping his own idiom into a genuinely organistic mode of expression, he will accept the challenge to put to effective use the color and ensemble resources of the organ.

---

[39]However, his significance as a unique organ composer is minimized by his compatriot Hodeir: ". . . Beneath his finger tips, the organ has a new sound for the first time since Franck; but then this may merely be the swan song of a once glorious instrument." André Hodeir, *Since Debussy, a View of Contemporary Music*, trans. Noel Birch. New York: Grove Press, 1961, p. 112.

[40]It is heartening, indeed, to observe the ever-increasing interest in church music by congregations at large. The last two decades have brought unprecedented developments. Active leadership and participation by the laity have resulted in unequalled opportunities. Here is one of the exciting challenges facing the church today.

[41]For a clear exposition of the characteristics of liturgical communication, see Romano Guardini, *The Spirit of the Liturgy*, trans. A. Lane. London: Sheed and Ward, 1930.

[42]This concept is not to be misconstrued as an apology for conservatism. On the contrary, it rests on the implicit condition of systematic, Sunday-by-Sunday church musical education of congregations. No musical limitations or qualifications other than liturgical functionalism are imposed.

It is the author's considered opinion that many pastors and church musicians are underestimating the musical intelligence of present-day congregations.

A third condition is the organist's recognition and acceptance of the practical aspect of improvised hymn elaborations. One of the main obstacles for present-day musicians is the liturgically required use of chorale or hymn tunes for contemporary musical expression. Quite apart from the fact that many musicians would prefer choosing their own thematic material, mandatory use of *cantus firmi* compels them to deal with musical materials of modal or tonal origin, a condition which is felt by many to be unacceptable for truly contemporary utterance. However, it is unlikely that congregational hymn singing will be replaced in the near future by some other usage. It is equally unlikely that musical utterance by the congregation could be cast into forms essentially dissimilar to present-day hymns and chorales. Therefore, the chorale elaboration will continue to be one of the vital factors of service playing.[43] Acceptance rather than rejection of the challenge to incorporate into thoroughly contemporary musical usage the modal or tonal aspects of hymns and chorales would seem to be the constructive answer to the dilemma.

Obviously, it becomes increasingly difficult to utilize effectively a chorale tune when a composer's idiom is so advanced as to show few if any points of affinity with tonal concepts.[44] An idiom which makes use of tonal centers—no matter how sophisticated—is more readily adaptable to chorale-based composing and especially to the chorale improvisation. However, this should not be interpreted as an invitation to indulge in dry, conventional textures which slavishly imitate bygone styles. A creative and intelligent approach to using hymn tunes in a provocative, fresh, and functional manner, free of stodgy pedantries, must be one of the organist's primary aims.[45]

Unfortunately, there are no easy ways to acquire such a style. To date, no definitive teaching method has introduced within the framework of tonality[46] entirely new avenues. Certain modifications of various concepts (parallelism, rhythmic treatment) may reflect more recent usage, but the basic conventions of the common practice period have remained intact. Thus, the student of organ improvisation should not hesitate to employ at first a conventional manner (see Examples II$_{22}$, II$_{25}$, II$_{26}$, II$_{28}$, II$_{29}$, II$_{30}$, II$_{33}$, II$_{35}$, II$_{36}$, II$_{37}$). As he gains confidence through much study and practice, his musical idiom will assume personal traits along with a less conventional syntax (see Examples II$_{23}$, II$_{24}$, II$_{27}$, II$_{31}$, II$_{32}$, II$_{34}$, II$_{38}$, II$_{39}$-II$_{42}$). Whether or not the organist's style is compatible with and expressive of contemporary thought depends in great measure on his ability to transform academically absorbed disciplines into lively and practical musical utterance. In order for his style to be liturgically suitable, the organist must possess above all sincerity of conviction in addition to such other necessary qualifications as excellent professional preparation, freshness and functionalism of approach, and a fine rapport with congregation and choir. Without conscious professional and theological foundation, music in the service all too easily turns hollow, pathetic, sweet, or even cute.[47] Improvisation, especially, transmits conviction or lack of it. The organist who continually rallies all of his talents to the humble service of the Most High has found the basic criterion for idiom and style. He will neither be a musical apologist nor an egocentric subjectivist. His esthetic, artistic, and creative objectives are employed to the end of returning his gifts to him, "of whom and through whom and to whom are all things."

---

[43]In the author's opinion, mere realization by the organist of this utilitarian necessity is not sufficient, as it is likely to produce only grudgingly rendered and, at best, competently handled improvisations. Hymnody, however, at its best is part of that aspect of the church's heritage which transcends the limits of time. In order to produce musically convincing chorale improvisations, the organist must feel "in tune" with this heritage, considering its practice a privilege rather than an impediment. It should be remembered that Bach's use of the chorale bespeaks his fullest acceptance of and unreserved identification with Lutheran hymnody as a key factor within his musical language.

[44]While it is not difficult to find examples of contemporary music based on chants, chorales, or folk tunes in the works of composers like Bartok, Hindemith, Messiaen, Stravinsky, and others using non-serial approaches, such instances become rather rare in serialism. However, Berg (in his *Violin Concerto*) and Schönberg (in the third movement of his *Suite for Clarinets, Strings and Pianoforte, op.* 22) have demonstrated that a combination of tonal elements with concepts of serialism is not altogether unfeasible.

[45]In the author's opinion the reluctance to deal with hymn and chorale tunes is not always based on considerations of idiom and style alone. Frequently it is the composer's fear of being identified with non-modern and unfashionable usage and his antipathy to being typecast by his colleagues and the general public, which keep him from contributing to hymn-related organ literature.

[46]For a fascinating approach to serial improvisation, see William Hibbard's "Some Aspects of Serial Improvisation," *American Guild of Organists Quarterly*, XI/4 (1966) and XII/1 (1967).

[47]Stravinsky states flatly: "Religious music without religion is almost always vulgar." Igor Stravinsky and Robert Craft, *Conversations with Igor Stravinsky.* Garden City, N.Y.: Doubleday, 1959, p. 142.

Chapter 7

CONCLUSION

The preceding chapters represent an attempt to outline practical methods of chorale improvisation. No definitive answers to the problems facing the contemporary church musician are proposed, nor should the suggested methods and the described types of improvised hymn treatment be considered unalterable and/or final. Indeed, this book will have served its purpose if it can be of some aid to the organist in the systematic exploration of improvisation.

Once again, it must be stressed that improvisation is a form of composing. Within the liturgical framework, it supplies that element of freshness and spontaneity which is essential to the organic flow of the service. While it should not be confused with careless meandering or with halting and incoherent utterance, its lively pulse is as necessary for the immediacy of service music as is the carefully practiced rendition of an organ work. The aspiring improviser should therefore not hesitate to begin by writing out beforehand parts or all of his improvisations. Gradually he will gain confidence and will succeed in freeing himself from his dependence on notation. Hard work and infinite patience will eventually yield results.

On the other hand, improvisation—like so many facets of church musical practice—will fail its liturgical objective whenever it becomes an end in itself rather than an agent of humble service. The organist must guard against becoming so engrossed in the mechanics of improvisation as to begin displaying his own artfulness and virtuosity, rather than making them subservient to the liturgical purpose. He should not become so preoccupied with his improvisations as to displace from the service worthy works by masters of the past as well as by contemporary writers. It should be remembered that even Bach played and performed music—often inferior to his own—by his contemporaries whenever he could obtain it. His concept of a "regulated church music to the glory of God" is as relevant today as it was in the eighteenth century. The only legitimate objective can be the lively response of the Christian to the *kerygma* through the best and most appropriate musical means available.

This regulated music aspires to the lofty goal of speaking with and for the congregation to God himself, setting the proper tone and inducing the appropriate attitude. The organist's weighty responsibility, whether he is playing for high festival services or for some scantily attended midweek Vespers, remains the same: *Laudate Deum in Chordis et Organo*. At no time should he ever succumb to routine. The psalmist's emphasis on the quality of newness in calling for that "*canticum novum*" must be his continual source of encouragement for freshness and newness of approach and an ever present admonition for careful and intelligent improvisation in Bach's spirit, "*Deo Soli Gloria*."

APPENDICES

APPENDIX I

Selected Chorales for Additional Study and Practice

"Mit Freuden zart"
Geneva (1551)

"Steht auf, ihr lieben Kinderlein"
Nikolaus Herman (1561)

"O Heiland, reiss die Himmel auf"
Augsburg (1665)

"Auf, auf, ihr Reichsgenossen"
Thomas Selle (1651)

"Da Christus geboren war"
(1544)

"Ich weiss, woran ich glaube"   Heinrich Schütz (1628)

6.

"Kommt und lasst uns Christum ehren"   (14th. century)

7.

"Das alte Jahr"   Johann Steurlein (1588)

8.

"Ich freu mich in dem Herren"   Bartholomaeus Helder (1648)

9.

"O Christe, Morgensterne"   Bartholomaeus Gesius (1605)

10.

"Es sind doch selig" or "O Mensch bewein"

Matthias Greitter (1525)

11.

"Du grosser Schmerzensmann"

Martin Jan (1663)

12.

"Sei Lob und Ehr"

Lyon 1597, Johann Crüger (1653)

13.

"Heut singt die liebe Christenheit"

Nikolaus Herman (1560)

14.

"Wohl denen, die da wandeln"

Heinrich Schütz (1628)

15.

APPENDIX II

Reference Material

Far from being comprehensive, the following compilations are intended as aids to the student who wishes to inquire further into improvisational techniques.

Appendix II-A: List of selected organ works whose texture and appearance suggest improvisation as chief originative factor.

Bach, Johann Christoph. *44 Choräle zum Präambulieren.* Ed. Martin Fischer. Kassel: Bärenreiter, 1948.

Bach, Johann Sebastian.	*Peters*	*BWV*	*NBA*
"Allein Gott in der Höh"	VI.3	711	IV,3.P.11
"Allein Gott in der Höh"	IX.14	715	IV,3.P.14
"Gelobet seist du, Jesu Christ"	V,Anh.1	722	IV,3.P.31
"Herr Jesu Christ, dich zu uns wend"	IX.18	726	IV,3.P.45
"In dulci jubilo"	V,Anh.3	729	IV,3.P.52
"Jesus, meine Zuversicht"	V,Anh.2	728	IV,3.P.58
"Lobt Gott, ihr Christen, allzugleich"	V,Anh.6	732	IV,3.P.64
"Wer nur den lieben Gott lässt walten"	V.52	691	IV,3.P.98

Peters=C. F. Peters, N.Y.
BWV=Bach Werke Verzeichnis (Schmieder).
NBG=Neue Bachgesellschaft. Kassel: Bärenreiter.

Böhm, Georg. "Herr Jesu Christ, dich zu uns wend," *Sämtliche Werke: Klavier-und Orgelwerke*, II. Ed. Johannes Wolgast; newly ed. Gesa Wolgast. Wiesbaden: Breitkopf & Härtel, 1952.

Buxtehude, Dietrich. "Wie schön leuchtet der Morgenstern," *Orgelwerke.* Ed. Philipp Spitta; newly ed. Max Seiffert, III. Wiesbaden: Breitkopf & Härtel, 1952.

Clokey, Joseph W. *Thirty-five Interludes on Hymn Tunes.* Glen Rock, N.J.: J. Fischer, 1958.

David, Johann Nepomuk. "Macht hoch die Tür, die Tor macht weit: Kleine Partita, II," *Choralwerk*, II. Wiesbaden: Breitkopf & Härtel, 1932.

Fischer, Johann Kaspar Ferdinand. *Blumenstrauss.* Ed. Rudolf Walter. 3rd ed. Altötting: Alfred Coppenrath, 1956.

Kastner, Macario Santiago, ed. *Altitalienische Versetten für Orgel oder andere Tasteninstrumente.* Mainz: B. Schott's Söhne, 1957.

Kerll, Johann Kaspar. *Modulatio Organica.* Ed. Rudolf Walter. Altötting: Alfred Coppenrath, 1956.

Krapf, Gerhard. "II Partita . . . Quod divina voluit clementia: Flessibile," *Historia Nativitatis: A Christmas Sonata da Chiesa on Three Chorales.* Glen Rock, N.J.: J. Fischer, 1962.

Lübeck, Vincent. "Zugabe: Lobt Gott ihr Christen allzugleich," *Klavier-Übung, 1728.* Ed. Hilmar Trede. New York, N.Y.: C. F. Peters, 1941.

Micheelsen, Hans-Friedrich. *Organistenpraxis.* 2 vols. Hamburg: Hüllenhagen & Griehl, 1952.

Musikgeschichtliche Kommission, E. V. "Komm, heiliger Geist (anon.)," "Gelobet seist du, Jesu Christ," "Christe, der du bist Tag und Licht," *Das Erbe deutscher Musik, Abteilung Orgel, Klavier, Laute: Die Lüneburger Orgeltabulatur KN 208*, XXXVI. Ed. Margarete Reimann. Frankfurt: Henry Litolff's Verlag, 1957.

Nelson, Ronald A. *Hymntune Sketches.* Minneapolis, Minn.: Augsburg Publishing House, 1963.

Pachelbel, Johann. "Anhang," *Johann Christoph Bach, 44 Choräle zum Präambulieren.* Ed. Martin Fischer. Kassel: Bärenreiter, 1948.

Pachelbel, Wilhelm Hieronymous. "O Lamm Gottes unschuldig," *Werke für Orgel und Clavier, Gesamtausgabe*. Eds. Hans Joachim Moser and Traugott Fedtke. Kassel: Bärenreiter, 1957.

Peeters, Flor. *Thirty Short Preludes on Well-known Hymns, for Organ, op*. 95. New York: C. F. Peters, 1960.

Pepping, Ernst. "Es kommt ein Schiff geladen," *Kleines Orgelbuch*. Mainz: B. Schott's Söhne, 1944.

———— "Die ganze Welt," *Zwölf Choralvorspiele*. Kassel: Bärenreiter, 1957.

Rohlig, Harald. *Partita on the Chorale "Ah, Holy Jesus."* Minneapolis, Minn.: Augsburg Publishing House, 1963.

Scheidt, Samuel. Bicinia in Hymns "A solis ortus cardine," "Christe, qui lux es et dies," "Vita Sanctorum, Decus Angelorum," "O Lux beata Trinitas," *Tabulatura Nova*, III. Ed. Christhard Mahrenholz. Hamburg: Ugrino Verlag, 1928.

Speuy, Henderick. *Psalm Preludes for Organ or Harpsichord*. Ed. Frits Noske. Amsterdam: Edition Heuwekemeijer, 1963.

Walcha, Helmut. "Den die Hirten lobten sehre," *Fünfundzwanzig Choralvorspiele für Orgel*. Frankfurt: C. F. Peters, 1954.

Appendix II-B: Selected list of works illustrative of free hymn accompaniment and/or of the *alternatim* organ stanza.

Bach, Johann Sebastian. *Orgelbüchlein*. (BWV 599-644.)

Bender, Jan. *Festival Preludes on Six Chorales*. St. Louis, Mo.: Concordia Publishing House, 1963. Foreword by Paul Thomas.

———— *Tabulatura Americana, Organ Settings*. 3 vols. St. Louis, Mo.: Concordia Publishing House, 1961-63.

Bornefeld, Helmut. *Begleitsätze für Tasten- oder Melodieinstrumente zum Gemeindechor- oder Einzelgesang (auch als Orgelchoräle zu gebrauchen)*. Kassel: Bärenreiter, 1950——.

Caine, Myran. *A First Book of Hymns for the Beginning Organist*. St. Louis, Mo.: Concordia Publishing House, 1964.

Coleman, Henry. *Varied Hymn Accompaniments*. London: Oxford University Press, 1953.

Free Organ Accompaniments to Festival Hymns. 3 vols. Minneapolis, Minn.: Augsburg Publishing House, 1963-66.

Gerok, Karl and Hans Arnold Metzger. *Neues Choralbuch zum Evangelischen Kirchengesangbuch*. Kassel: Bärenreiter, 1956.

Krapf, Gerhard. "Psalmodia Evangelica," II, III; "A solis ortus cardine," III, IV; "Christ lag in Todesbanden," III, IV; "Komm, Heiliger Geist, Herre Gott," II, III; "St. Anne," III, IV; *Organ Vespers*. Minneapolis, Minn.: Augsburg Publishing House, 1964.

Noble, T. Tertius. *Free Organ Accompaniments to One Hundred Well-known Hymn Tunes*. Glen Rock, N.J.: J. Fischer, 1946.

———— *Fifty Free Organ Accompaniments to Well-known Hymn Tunes*. Glen Rock, N.J.: J. Fischer, 1949.

Pepping, Ernst. "Wie soll ich dich empfangen," "Kommt und lasst uns Christum ehren," "Ich steh an deiner Krippen hier," "Gottes Sohn ist kommen," "O wir armen Sünder," "O, Traurigkeit, o Herzeleid," "O Haupt voll Blut und Wunden," "Auf, auf mein Herz, mit Freuden," "Mit Freuden zart," "Gelobt sei Gott im höchsten Thron," "Ach wundergrosser Siegesheld (with optional unison voices)," *Grosses Orgelbuch*. 3 vols. Mainz: B. Schott's Söhne, 1941.

Rohlig, Harald. *Thirty New Settings of Familiar Hymn Tunes*. New York, N.Y.: Abingdon Press, 1963.

Scheidt, Samuel. *Das Görlitzer Tabulaturbuch, 1650*. Ed. Christhard Mahrenholz. New York, N.Y.: C. F. Peters, 1940.

Appendix II-C: Selected bibliography to Chapter 5 (Selection of works is not limited to improvisations only, since the main purpose of this compilation is furnishing additional references for analytical studies of contrapuntal and formal aspects. Works listed in appendixes II-A and II-B have been omitted; however, practical editions of works represented in II-A and II-B have been included for the benefit of the student who wishes to acquire selected works for performance purposes.)

Andrews, Bennett. *Changes on Three Hymn Tunes*. New York, N.Y.: J. Fischer, 1953.

Bach, Johann Sebastian. *Orgelwerke*. Ed. F. K. Griepenkerl sen., V, VI, VII. New York: C. F. Peters, 1844.

Baumgartner, H. Leroy. *Seven Preludes on Familiar Hymn Tunes for Organ*. Glen Rock, N.J.: J. Fischer, 1957.

Bender, Jan. *Kleine Choralvorspiele*. 3 vols. Kassel: Bärenreiter, 1961-63.

Benoit, Dom Paul, O.S.B. *Esquisses Liturgiques*. Glen Rock, N.J.: J. Fischer, 1958.

Boeringer, James. *Prelude on "O Sacred Head."* Minneapolis, Minn.: Augsburg Publishing House, 1964.

Brahms, Johannes. *Eleven Chorale Preludes, op*. 122. Ed. E. Power Biggs. New York: Mercury Music Corp., 1949.

———— *Organ Works*. Eds. Walter E. Buszin and Paul Bunjes. 2 vols. and supplement. New York: C. F. Peters, 1964.

Buszin, Walter E. ed. *Anthology of Sacred Music*. 3 vols. St. Louis, Mo.: Concordia Publishing House, 1948-50.

Buxtehude, Dietrich. *Orgelwerke.* Ed. Philipp Spitta. Newly ed. Max Seiffert, III, IV. Wiesbaden: Breitkopf & Härtel, 1952.

———— *Sämtliche Orgelwerke.* Ed. Joseph Hedar. III, IV. Copenhagen: Wilhelm Hansen, 1952.

Candlyn, T. F. H. *Prelude on "Divinum Mysterium."* New York: H. W. Gray, 1930.

Cassler, G. Winston. *Hymntune Preludes for the Organ.* 4 vols. Minneapolis, Minn.: Augsburg Publishing House, 1960-62.

———— *Organ Music for the Church Year.* Minneapolis, Minn.: Augsburg Publishing House, 1959.

Clokey, Joseph W. *Ten Meditations on Hymn Melodies.* Glen Rock, N.J.: J. Fischer, 1954.

Couperin, Francois. *Oeuvres complètes: Musique d'orgue.* Ed. Maurice Cauchie. Paris: Editions de l'Oiseau-Lyre, Louise B. M. Dyer, 1932. VI.

Crane, Robert. *Five Baroque Chorale Preludes.* St. Louis, Mo.: Concordia Publishing House, 1955.

Daquin, Louis Claude. *New Book of Noels.* Ed. E. Power Biggs. 2 vols. New York: Mercury Music Corp., 1947-48.

———— Nouveau Livre de Noels, *Archives des maitres de l'orgue*, III/5. Ed. Felix Alexandre Guilmant, and André Pirro, 1903-1907. Schott reprint, n.d.

Darke, Harold. *A Meditation on "Brother James's Air."* London: Oxford Univ. Press, 1948.

David, Johann Nepomuk. *Choralwerk.* 15 vols. Wiesbaden: Breitkopf & Härtel, 1932-1962.

Davis, William R. *Two Chorale Preludes.* New York: H. W. Gray, 1964.

DeKlerk, Albert. *Octo Fantasiae super themata Gregoriana pro organo.* Utrecht: Wed. J. R. van Rossum, 1954.

Dickinson, Peter. *Postlude on Adeste Fideles.* London: Novello, 1964.

Dressler, John. *Twelve Choral-Preludes on Great Hymns of the Church.* Glen Rock, N.J.: J. Fischer, 1962.

Dupré, Marcel. *Sixteen Chorales (Le Tombeau de Titelouse).* New York: H. W. Gray, 1950 (copyright assigned by S. Bornemann, Paris).

———— *Variations sur un Noël.* Paris: Alphonse Leduc, 1923.

Duro, John. *Six Contemplations, Improvisations on familiar hymns.* New York: H. W. Gray, 1954.

———— *Variations on "I Saw Three Ships."* New York: H. W. Gray, 1961.

Dyson, George. *Variations on Old Psalm-Tunes.* 3 vols. London: Novello, 1960-61.

Edmundson, Garth. *From the Western Church, Seven Preludes for Organ.* New York: H. W. Gray, 1954.

———— *Seven Classic Preludes on Old Chorales.* Glen Rock, N.J.: J. Fischer, 1938.

Fleischer, Heinrich, ed. *The Parish Organist.* 12 vols. St. Louis, Mo.: Concordia Publishing House, 1953. I-IV. Ed. Erich Goldschmidt, 1955-56, V-VIII. Ed. Thomas Gieschen, 1962, IX-X. Ed. Willem Mudde, 1966, XI-XII.

Frescobaldi, Girolamo. *Fiori Musicali (1635): Ausgewählte Orgelwerke*, I. Ed. Hermann Keller. New York: C. F. Peters, 1943.

Gigault, Nicolas. *Livre de Musique pour l'orgue, Archives des maitres de l'orgue.* Ed. Felix Alexandre Guilmant and André Pirro, 1903-1907, IV. Schott reprint, n.d.

Graf, Adolf, ed. *Choralvorspiele für den gottesdienstlichen Gebrauch.* 2nd ed. Kassel: Bärenreiter, 1939.

Grigny, Nicolas de. *Livre d'orgue, Archives des maitres de l'orgue.* Ed. Felix Alexandre Guilmant and André Pirro, 1903-1907, V/1. Schott reprint, n.d.

Groom, Lester. *Two Compositions for Organ.* Nashville, Tenn.: Abingdon Press, 1964.

Haag, Herbert and Walter Hennig, eds. *Neue Orgelvorspiele zu wenig bearbeiteten Liedern des Evangelischen Kirchengesangbuches.* Berlin: Verlag Merseburger, 1961.

Haase, Karl. *Preludes for the Hymns of the Lutheran Hymnal.* 4 vols. Lincoln, Nebraska: Karl Haase, 1948-49.

Hays, Robert Wilson. *Improvisation (On a Plainsong Melody).* New York: H. W. Gray, 1956.

Heussenstamm, George. *Our Father, Thou in Heaven Above; Partita.* St. Louis, Mo.: Concordia Publishing House, 1964.

Hokanson, Margrethe. *Seven Improvisations on Hymns and Folk Tunes.* Minneapolis, Minn.: Augsburg Publishing House, 1959.

———— *Six Chorale Improvisations for Organ.* Minneapolis, Minn.: Augsburg Publishing House, 1938.

Jaques, Robert. *Prelude on a Fifteenth Century Carol.* New York: H. W. Gray, 1963.

Kauder, Hugo. *Three Preludes on Gregorian Hymns.* Boston: E. C. Schirmer, 1963.

Kauffmann, Georg Friedrich. *Harmonische Seelenlust.* Ed. Pierre Pidoux. Kassel: Bärenreiter, 1951.

Kee, Cor. *Merck toch hoe sterck con variazioni. Niewe Nederlandsche Orgelmuziek*, XXX. Amsterdam: G. Alsbach, n.d.

———— *Psalmen voor Orgel, Nieuwe Nederlandsche Orgelmuziek* XXVI-XXVIII. Amsterdam: G. Alsbach, n.d.

Keller, Hermann, ed. *80 Chorale Preludes, German Masters of the 17th and 18th Centuries, Organ.* New York: C. F. Peters, 1951.

Krapf, Gerhard. *Partita "Mit Freuden Zart."* St. Louis, Mo.: Concordia Publishing House, 1965.

———— *Partita "Lobe den Herren"* St. Louis, Mo.: Concordia Publishing House, 1966.

Lacey, David T. *Prelude on "Georgetown."* New York: H. W. Gray, 1964.

Lang, C. S. *Twenty Hymn-Tune Preludes.* Fair Lawn, N.J.: Oxford University Press, 1963.

Lapo, Cecil E. *Four Organ Preludes on Chorale Tunes.* Nashville, Tenn.: Abingdon Press, 1965.

Lenel, Ludwig. *Four Organ Chorales.* St. Louis, Mo.: Concordia Publishing House, 1958.

Leupold, Anton Wilhelm. *Orgelbuch.* Ed. Ulrich Leupold. Berlin: Verlag Merseburger, 828. This is a selected reprint of *Orgelbuch.* 4 vols. Wolfenbuettel: Georg Kallmeyer Verlag, 1933 (now out of print). Chantry Music Press Ltd., Fremont, Ohio, has issued an American edition: *An Organ Book.*

Maekelberghe, August. *Plainsong Prelude.* New York: H. W. Gray, 1961.

Mathias, William. *Variations on a Hymn Tune.* London: Oxford University Press, 1963.

Matthews, H. Alexander. *Ten Choral Preludes and a Fantasy.* Bryn Mawr, Penn.: Theodore Presser/Oliver Ditson, 1949.

———— *Twelve Choral Preludes on Familiar Hymn Tunes.* Bryn Mawr, Penn.: Theodore Presser/Oliver Ditson, 1946.

Means, Claude. *Carol Prelude on "Joseph Dearest, Joseph Mine."* New York: H. W. Gray, 1964.

———— *Choral Prelude on "Down Ampney."* New York: H. W. Gray, 1959.

Meek, Kenneth. *Three Preludes on Plainsong Melodies.* New York: H. W. Gray, 1959.

Micheelsen, Hans Friedrich. *Choralmusik für Orgel.* Kassel: Bärenreiter, 1959.

Miles, Russell Hancock. *Two Lenten Chorale Preludes.* New York: H. W. Gray, 1964.

Novello & Co., ed. *Festal Voluntaries.* 6 vols. London: Novello, 1956.

Oley, J. C. *Four Chorale Preludes.* Ed. Walter Emery. London: Novello, 1958.

Oxford University Press, ed. *A Book of Hymn Tune Voluntaries.* London: Oxford Univ. Press, 1950.

Oxley, Harrison. *Two Carols for Organ.* London: Novello, 1963.

Pachelbel, Johann. *Ausgewählte Orgelwerke.* Ed. Karl Matthaei. Kassel: Bärenreiter, 1934-36, II-IV.

———— *Cent Nouveaux Versets de Magnificat.* Ed. Noël Pierront and Norbert Dufourc. I, II. Paris: Bornemann, 1958.

Peek, Richard. *Fantasia and Fugue on "St. Anne."* Charlotte, N.C.: Brodt Music Co., 1964.

————, ed. *Organ Music for Worship,* I. Charlotte, N.C.: Brodt Music Co., 1963.

———— *Prelude on a Theme by Tallis.* Charlotte, N.C.: Brodt Music Co., 1960.

Peeters, Flor. *Chorale Preludes, op. 68-70.* 3 vols. New York: C. F. Peters, 1950.

———— *Hymn Preludes for the Liturgical Year for Organ, op. 100.* vols. I-XII. New York: C. F. Peters, 1966.

———— *Hymn Preludes for the Liturgical Year for Organ, op. 100.* vols. XIII-XXIV. New York: C. F. Peters, 1967.

———— *30 Chorale Preludes on Gregorian Hymns, op. 75-77.* 3 vols. New York: C. F. Peters, 1954-56.

Pepping, Ernst. *Hymnen für Orgel.* Kassel: Bärenreiter, 1954.

Pfatteicher, Carl F. and Archibald T. Davison, ed. *The Church Organist's Golden Treasury.* 3 vols. Bryn Mawr, Penn.: Oliver Ditson, 1949-51.

Poppen, Hermann. *Vierzehn Choralvorspiele für Orgel zu neueren Liedern.* Mainz: B. Schott's Söhne, 1939.

Proctor, Robert E. *Prelude on "Ortonville."* Charlotte, N.C.: Brodt Music Co., 1964.

Read, Gardner. *Eight Preludes on Old Southern Hymns, op. 90.* New York: H. W. Gray, 1952.

———— *Six Preludes on Old Southern Hymns, op. 112.* New York: H. W. Gray, 1963.

Reda, Siegfried. *Choralvorspiele.* Kassel: Bärenreiter, 1954.

———— *Vorspiele zu den Psalmliedern des EKG.* Kassel: Bärenreiter, 1957.

Reger, Max. *Dreissig kleine Choralvorspiele, op. 135a.* Berlin: N. Simrock, G.m.b.H., 1915.

———— *Orgelwerke, op. 67: Zweiundfünfzig leicht ausführbare Vorspiele zu den gebräuchlichsten evangelischen Chorälen.* 3 vols. Berlin: Bote & Bock, 1903.

Rhea, Arthur D. *Prelude on "Intercessor."* New York: H. W. Gray, 1964.

Roberts, Myron J. *Improvisation on the Agincourt Hymn.* New York: H. W. Gray, 1964.

Rohr, Heinrich, ed. *Orgelspiel im Kirchenjahr.* Mainz: B. Schott's Söhne, 1951.

Saxton, Stanley E. *Chorale, Variation and Finale on "Now Thank We All Our God."* Charlotte, N.C.: Brodt Music Co., 1964.

———— *Prelude and Fugue on "Adeste Fideles."* Charlotte, N.C.: Brodt Music Co., 1964.

———— *Prelude on "Vater Unser."* Charlotte, N.C.: Brodt Music Co., 1964.

Schroeder, Hermann. *Die Marianischen Antiphone für Orgel.* Mainz: B. Schott's Söhne, 1954.

———— *Sechs Orgelchoräle, op.* 11. Mainz: B. Schott's Söhne, 1934.

Sessions, Roger, *Three Chorale Preludes.* New York: Edward B. Marks, 1934.

Simonds, Bruce. *Prelude on "Iam sol recedit igneus."* London: Oxford University Press, 1930.

Sowerby, Leo. *Meditations on Communion Hymns.* New York: H. W. Gray, 1942.

———— *Prelude on "Land of Rest," Prelude on "Were You There?"* New York: H. W. Gray, 1956.

Straube, Karl, ed. *Choralvorspiele alter Meister.* New York: C. F. Peters, 1907.

Sweelinck, Jan Pieter. *Ausgewählte Werke für Orgel und Klavier: Choralbearbeitungen,* II. Ed. Diethard Hellmann. New York: C. F. Peters, 1957.

Telemann, Georg Philipp. *Twelve Easy Chorale Preludes.* Ed. Hermann Keller. New York: C. F. Peters, 1951.

Thomson, Virgil. *Pange lingua for Organ.* New York: G. Schirmer, 1962.

Titcomb, Everett. *Benedicta Tu.* New York: H. W. Gray, 1953.

———— *Improvisation on the Eighth Psalm Tone.* New York: H. W. Gray, 1959.

Trevor, C. H., ed. *Seasonal Chorale Preludes.* 2 vols. London: Oxford University Press, 1963.

Triplett, Robert F. *Organ Chorale: O God, Thou Faithful God.* Nashville, Tenn.: Abingdon Press, 1964.

Tunder, Franz. *Sämtliche Choralbearbeitungen für Orgel.* Ed. Rudolf Walter. Mainz: B. Schott's Söhne, 1958.

Van Hulse, Camil. *Seven Preludes on Advent Hymns.* St. Louis, Mo.: Concordia Publishing House, 1952.

———— *Seven Preludes on Christmas Hymns.* St. Louis, Mo.: Concordia Publishing House, 1952.

———— *Seven Preludes on Hymns for Easter.* St. Louis, Mo.: Concordia Publishing House, 1955.

———— *Ten Preludes for Organ, Based on Well-known Hymn Tunes.* Glen Rock, N.J.: J. Fischer, 1954.

Walter, Samuel. *Nine Compositions for Organ.* Nashville, Tenn.: Abingdon Press, 1955.

Walther, Johann Gottfried. *A Collection of Chorale Preludes.* Ed. Theodore Beck. St. Louis, Mo.: Concordia Publishing House, 1963.

———— *Gesammelte Werke für Orgel.* Ed. Max Seiffert. Leipzig: Breitkopf & Härtel, 1906.

Webber, Loyd. *Six Interludes on Passion Hymns.* London: Novello, 1964.

Wetherill, Edward H. *Five Seasonal Chorale Preludes.* Bryn Mawr, Penn.: Theodore Presser, 1965.

Willan, Healey. *36 Short Preludes and Postludes on Well-known Hymn Tunes for Organ.* 3 vols. New York: C. F. Peters, 1960.

Williams, David A. *Meditation on "Pange lingua."* New York: H. W. Gray, 1959.

Wright, Searle. *Prelude on "Brother James's Air."* London: Oxford University Press, 1958.

Wyton, Alec. *Fanfare—Improvisation on "Azmon."* Nashville, Tenn.: Abingdon Press, 1964.

APPENDIX III

Supplementary Exercises to Chapter 5

Hymn tune "Christus der ist mein Leben"   Melchior Vulpius (1609)

"Christus der ist mein Leben"
to Ex. II₂₆ (b)

"Christus der ist mein Leben"
to Ex. II₂₇ Adagio

"Christus der ist mein Leben"
to Ex. II₂₈(b) and II₂₈(d)

Hymn tune "Ich weiss, mein Gott, dass all mein Tun" Dresden (1608)

"Ich weiss, mein Gott, dass all mein Tun"

Add left hand to scheme given. Try different c.f. entries in right hand;
to Ex. II₂₉(b)   keep c.f. ostinato in pedal without interruption.

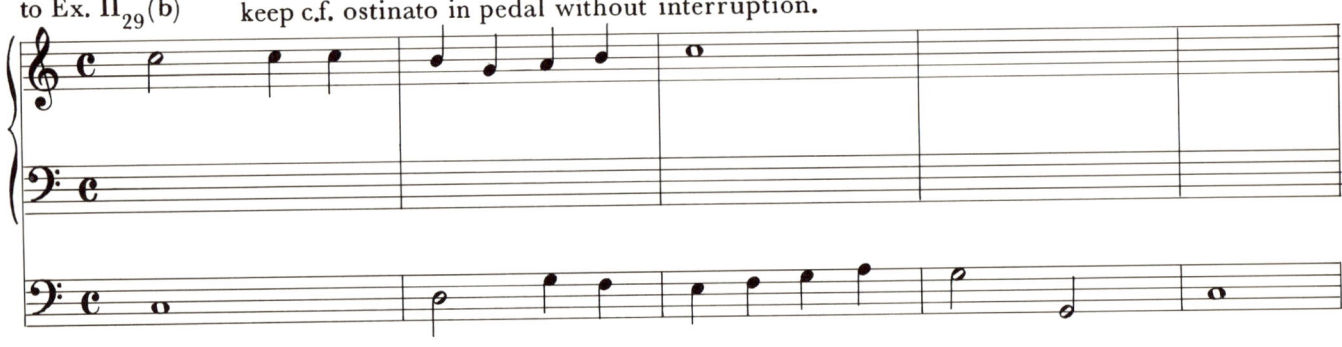

Hymn tune "Was Gott tut, das ist wohlgetan"

Severus Gastorius (1681)

"Was Gott tut, das ist wohlgetan"

to Ex. II$_{31}$(b) and II$_{31}$(d) Add one or two parts to given scheme; exchange voices for the repeat.

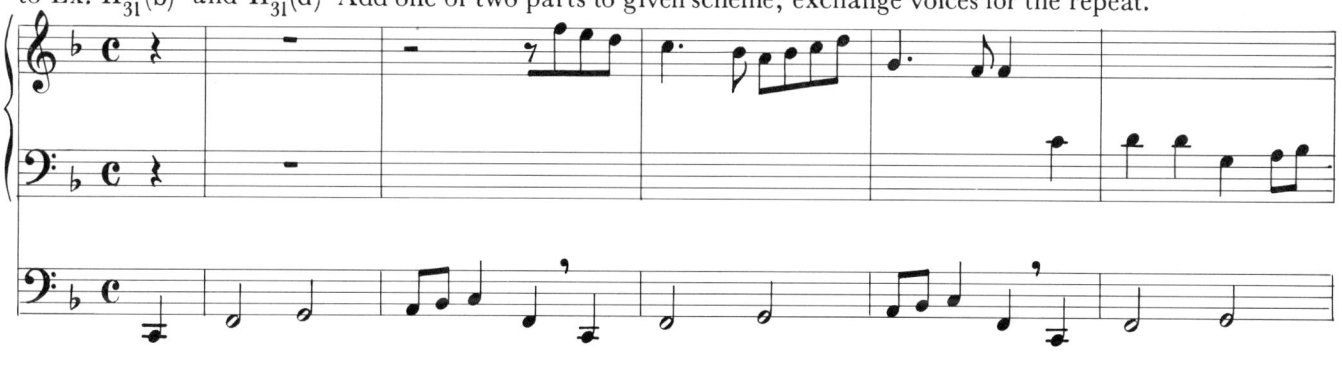

Hymn tune "Ich dank dir schon"

Moravia (1595)

"Ich dank dir schon"

to Ex. II$_{32}$(b) and II$_{32}$(d)

(Ped.)

Hymn tune "Werde munter"

Johann Schop (1642)

Ⓐ

Ⓑ   Ⓒ

"Werde munter"

At Ⓐ ritornello should be tranposed to g (see below); at Ⓑ
ritornello should be transposed to B♭; ritornelli preceding
all other c.f. lines may remain in F (transposition to d at Ⓒ is optional).

to Ex. II$_{33}$(b)

Hymn tune "Wie lieblich ist der Maien"

Johann Steurlein (1575)

"Wie lieblich ist der Maien"

to Ex. II₃₄(b), II₃₅(b), II₃₅(d)

c.f.

Hymn tune "Lobet den Herrn und dankt"

Johann Crüger (1640)

"Lobet den Herrn und dankt"

to Ex. II₃₆(b)

Add inner voice

16' or 8' basis

Hymn tune "Auf meinen lieben Gott"

Bartholomaeus Gesius (1605)

"Auf meinen lieben Gott"

to Ex. II₃₇(b)   Play *comes* with distance of two quarter notes

(Dux)

(Comes)

16' or 8' basis   (c.f.)

Hymn tune "O Lebensbrünnlein tief und gross"

Leipzig (1603)

Ⓐ   Ⓑ

Ⓒ   Ⓓ

Ⓔ   Ⓕ

"O Lebensbrünnlein tief und gross"

to Ex. II₃₈(b)

Use preimitations sketched below. Quote c.f. in half notes. Line Ⓑ may modulate to A major. Line Ⓔ may conclude in Phrygian cadence. c.f. to be played in pedal.

Preimitation to Ⓐ

107

Preimitation
to Ⓔ

Preimitation to Ⓕ

un poco rit.   *a tempo*

Phrygian
cadence
conclusion of Ⓔ

Hymn tune "Schwing dich auf zu deinem Gott"

Johann Crüger (1653)

"Schwing dich auf zu deinem Gott"

Plan schemes of preimitation for individual c.f. lines as shown in preceding example.
Note change of meter in last line of hymn tune.

to Ex. II₃₉

Moderato   c.f.

Hymn tune "Herzlich tut mich erfreuen"

(16th century)

"Herzlich tut mich erfreuen"

to Ex. II$_{40}$

Lightly

Hymn tune "O dass ich tausend Zungen hätte"

Balthasar König (1738)

"O dass ich tausend Zungen hätte"

to Ex. II$_{41}$(b)   Supply harmonization

Moderato

Ped. optional

109

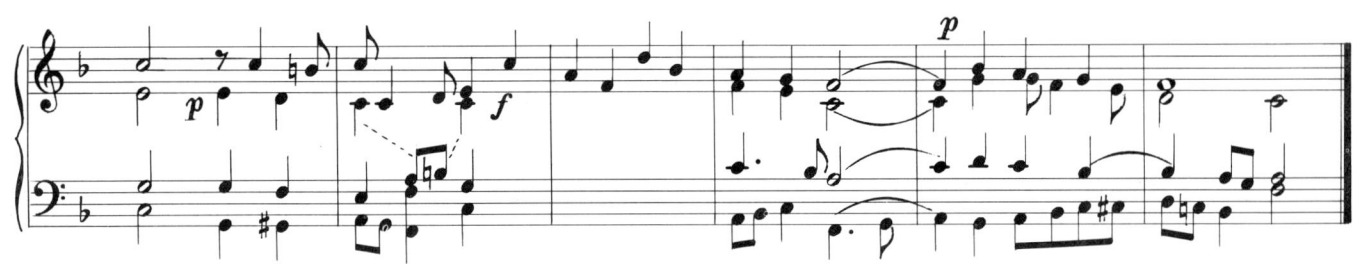

APPENDIX IV

[Note: Composers other than the author are identified in parentheses. Hymn tunes marked with an asterisk are found in five or more of the following hymnals.]

Baptist Hymnal (Southern Baptist Convention). Ed. Walter Hines Sims. Nashville, Tenn.: Convention Press, 1956.

Christian Worship (Northern Baptist Convention and Disciples of Christ). Philadelphia: The Judson Press, 1953.

The Harvard University Hymn Book. Ed. Samuel H. Miller and John Ferris. Cambridge, Mass.: Harvard University Press, 1964.

The Hymnal (Presbyterian Church in the U.S.A.). Philadelphia: Presbyterian Board of Education, 1938.

Hymnal for Colleges and Schools. Ed. Harold Geer. New Haven: Yale University Press, 1956.

The Hymnal of the Evangelical Mission Covenant Church of America. Chicago: Covenant Press, 1950.

The Hymnal of the Protestant Episcopal Church in the U.S.A. New York: The Church Pension Fund, 1940.

The Hymnbook. (Presbyterian and Reformed Churches). Richmond, Va.: John Ribble, 1955.

The Lutheran Hymnal (The Evangelical Lutheran Synodical Conference of North America). Saint Louis, Mo.: Concordia Publishing House, 1941.

The Methodist Hymnal. Nashville, Tenn.: Methodist Publishing House, 1966.

Pilgrim Hymnal, 8th ed. Boston: Pilgrim Press, 1962.

Service Book and Hymnal (Lutheran Churches). Minneapolis, Minn.: Augsburg Publishing House, 1958.

Songs of Praise. Ed. Percy Dearmer and Ralph Vaughan Williams. London: Oxford University Press, 1931.

Classified Index of Hymn Tunes

USABLE AS:

Hymn Tune and Key	Example	Short Introduction	Hymn Prelude	Congregational or Choral Accompaniment	Alternatim Stanza	Offertory, Postlude, etc.
*Allein Gott in der Höh; G	II 25	X		X	X	
Aus meines Herzens Grunde; F	II 31b	X				
Bonn. See Warum sollt ich mich denn grämen.						
Christus, der uns selig macht; Phrygian (G. F. Kauffmann)	II 35d		X			X
Das alte Jahr vergangen ist; G	I 1			X	X	X
Die güldne Sonne; F	II 40b				X	X
*Dundee, FRENCH; E♭	II 36b		X		X	X
Ebeling. See: Warum sollt ich mich denn grämen.						
*Erhalt uns, Herr, bei deinem Wort; e	I 6			X	X	
*Es ist ein Ros entsprungen; F	II 29b		X		X	X
	II 30 (for violin and harpsichord)					
Es kommt ein Schiff geladen; Dorian (E. Pepping)	II 32d		X			X
*Freu dich sehr, o meine Seele; G (J. G. Walther)	II 28d		X			X
*Gelobt sei Gott im höchsten Thron; D	I 5			X	X	
Geneva 42. See: Freu dich sehr, o meine Seele						
Gib Fried, o frommer, treuer Gott; Phrygian (S. Scheidt)	I 3			X	X	X
*Gott des Himmels; G	II 38b		X			X
Grosser Gott. See: Hursley	(By repeating measures 1-8 of Ex. II 41b, "Hursley," one may use it for "Grosser Gott.")					
*Hamburg; F	II 26b		X	X	X	X
	II 39					X
Herr Christ, der einig Gotts Sohn; F (S. Scheidt)	I 2			X	X	X
*Herzliebster Jesu; g	II 19b	X				
	II 24a	X		X	X	
	II 24b	X		X	X	
	II 27		X			X
*Hursley; F	II 41b		X	X	X	X
*Hyfrydol; F	II 35b		X			X

112

Hymn Tune and Key	Example	Short Introduction	Hymn Prelude	Congregational or Choral Accompaniment	Alternatim Stanza	Offertory, Postlude, etc.
*Jesu, meine Freude; d (F. W. Zachow)	I 7		X		X	X
Lobt Gott getrost mit Singen; G	I 4			X	X	X
*Morgenglanz der Ewigkeit	II 37b		X			X
*Nicaea	II 21b			X		
	II 21c			X	X	
	II 21d	X		X	X	X
	II 21e	X		X	X	X
Neumark. See: Wer nur den lieben Gott lässt walten						
O Jesu Christ, dein Kripplein ist. See: Wir Christenleut						
*O Jesu Christ, meins Lebens Licht; G	II 28b		X			
*O Jesu Christe, wahres Licht. See: O Jesu Christ, meins Lebens Licht						
Praetorius. See: Es ist ein Ros entsprungen						
Rosa mystica. See: Es ist ein Ros entsprungen						
Sleepers, Wake. See: Wachet auf						
Spires. See: Erhalt uns, Herr, bei deinem Wort						
*Stephanos; G	II 20c	X				
	II 20d	X				
*Stuttgart; G	II 33b		X			
Te Deum. See: Grosser Gott						
Wach auf, wach auf, du deutsches Land; D	II 42					X
*Wachet auf; C	II 18b	X				
	II 23a	X		X	X	
	II 23b	X		X	X	
*Warum sollt ich mich denn grämen; F	II 34b		X			X
*Wer nur den lieben Gott lässt walten; g (J. N. David)	II 31d		X			X
Wir Christenleut han jetzund Freud; E♭	II 32b	X				X
Wir warten dein, O Gottes Sohn; E♭	II 17b	X				
	II 17d	X				
	II 17e	X				
	II 22		X		X	X
Wolder. See: Aus meines Herzens Grunde.						

INDEX

The symbol (°) in front of a page number indicates a musical example.
The symbol (n) following a page number indicates a footnote.